Ooo-ee

ting ting

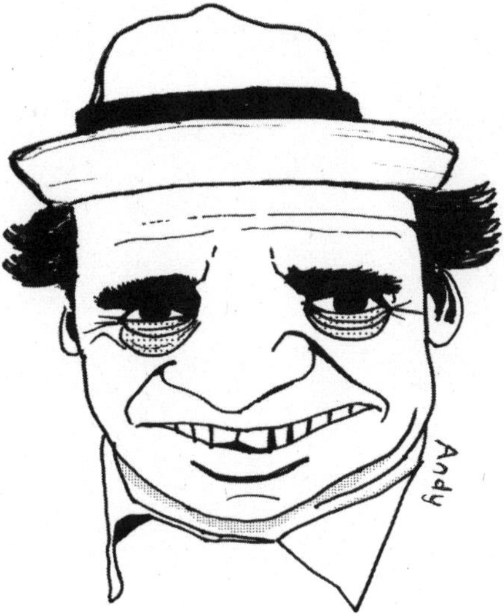
Andy

WALLOWING IN OUR OWN WELTSCHMERZ

WALLOWING IN OUR OWN WELTSCHMERZ

Andy Davidson, Chris Orton,
Andrew Orton, Robert Hammond,
and Matthew West

with illustrations by Andy X.Cable

miLLH

First published in Great Britain in 2014 by
Miwk Publishing Ltd
12 Marbles Way, Tadworth
Surrey KT20 5LW

Copyright © Auton 2014

'Doctor Who' series copyright © British Broadcasting Corporation

ISBN 978-1-908630-76-6

Cover art by Andrew Orton, photographs Mirrorpix and Phil MacD Photography

Cover design and book layout by Robert Hammond

Internal illustrations by Andy X. Cable

Printed and bound in Great Britain by TJ International, Padstow, Cornwall

This book is sold subject to the condition that it shall not, by way of trade or otherwise, be lent, resold, hired out or otherwise circulated without the publisher's prior written content in any form of binding or cover other than that in which it is published and without a similar condition including this condition being imposed on the subsequent publisher.

This book was lovingly Miwk made.

for Molly,
David and Bessie

Prologue

INTRODUCTION

This is a book of love.

We learned a long time ago that you can't make fun of something you don't love dearly. **Auton** has been poking fun of **Doctor Who** since 1989. Wait a minute! That's 25 years ago. Good grief. Have we still not grown up?

And yet stupidly, 25 years ago the programme we love, and love to make fun of, came off the air. How did we react? Well Robert started a fanzine: **Auton**. That's where we come from.

These days the kids with their baggy jeans, MP3s and iPhones have no idea what it was like to be a fan in the late eighties. Fandom turned its back on **Doctor Who**, led by fanatics who seemed to have forgotten they were fans and had become the enemy. We suspect fandom was a strong contributing factor to **Doctor Who**'s cancellation.

Some of us, not all of us, grew up on eighties **Doctor Who** and some of us, not all of us, enjoyed what we grew up with. One thing was clear, beyond *Time and the Rani* the show evolved, changed and became something new. It was sometimes silly, sometimes baffling, but always fun and always exciting. As we work our way through these twelve transmitted stories (and some other guff we've thrown in to beef up the page count) they don't seem as aged as *An Unearthly Child* was when they were aired. They still feel fresh. Sure, some of the effects are dated and maybe the incidental music is a bit enthusiastic in places (but still indicative of the time the show was made) and possibly the occasional performance is a bit off (when wasn't it in these fifty years?) but great heavens to crikey! It's good. <u>Good</u>.

We're about to pick some pretty substantial holes in some stories, throw out some ridiculous theories, consider some unlikely outcomes and play with reason and logic in plotting. But we're doing it out of love. We genuinely love this era. Why else would we choose it?

Why are we doing this? Well, several reasons actually. Firstly it's necessary for us, as a group, to get this out of our systems from time to time. Then there's the 25th anniversary. We have to do something, right? But finally there's the good cause.

Please read the book right to the end. We go into detail at the end of this book as to why we chose the charity we did. By purchasing this book you've helped that charity.

As we work on these books there's always this odd feeling that the physical product might survive for 150 years or more. Imagine someone in 2150AD thumbing the charity shop shelf and finding this. Poor sod.

Thank you. Please enjoy.

The Barely Consciousness.

The Bins Outside Television Centre
Wood Lane
W12 8QT

Dear Sirs,

I was going to issue you with a cease and desist letter to prevent publication of this obscene, inflammatory, unauthorised, baseless, inaccurate, loathsome, unwholesome, detestable, amateurish, pointless and scurrilous book dealing with my era as script editor on **Doctor Who**.

However, I found that this would involve a lawyer and would cost me money.

So we will now go for scenario number two. I want you to republish my out of print masterpiece **Script Doctor** in a deluxe new edition and pay me a ludicrously high royalty rate, or alternatively sell me boxes of the book at a knock down price so I can flog them at conventions.

Oh, wait a minute... you've already done that.

So, hang on, is this bloody book by you and Rob, Matt? Oh all right. Well that's okay then. I suppose you might as well just go ahead with it. I can even write you an introduction.

Just so long as I don't have to read the damned thing.

Nice pics, though.

Andrew Cartmel

There's many a slap twixt cup and a lap.
Old Gallifreyan Proverb

CONTENTMENTS

INTRODUCTION ... 13
(you already passed it)

FOREWORD BY ANDREW CARTMEL ... 15
(yup, passed that too)

CONTENTS ... 18
(you're looking at them)

SEASON 24

TIME AND THE RANI ... 23
(The one where the Tetrap resets a trap)

PARADISE TOWERS ... 35
(The one with the tablecloths)

DELTA AND THE BANNERMEN ... 53
(The one with all the honey)

DRAGONFIRE ... 67
(The one with the ice)

SEASON 25

REMEMBRANCE OF THE DALEKS ... 79
(The one with no Cybermen)

CONTENTMENTS CONTINUATED

THE HAPPINESS PATROL ... 99
(The one on Newsnight)

SILVER NEMESIS ... 115
(The one with the Nazis)

THE GREATEST SHOW IN THE GALAXY ... 133
(The one with the long title)

SEASON 26

BATTLEFIELD ... 149
(The one with the hot Czech chopper chick)

GHOST LIGHT ... 163
(The one without the hyphen)

THE CURSE OF FENRIC ... 175
(The one where Frank's got 'shore leave')

SURVIVAL ... 199
(The one with wall-to-wall pussy)

BEYOND THE SCHEDULE ... 217

Assorted page-filler.

Betty Grable!

Jane Russell!

Season 24

It all started in 1987.

The contracts to build EuroDisney are signed, Michael Jackson releases **Bad**, Lester Piggot is jailed for tax evasion, John Knoll completes the first edition of Photoshop, Starbucks begin their global takeover, Zac Efron, Karen Gillan and Dappy are all born, Liberace, Danny Kaye and Patrick Troughton pass away and **Three Men and a Baby** is the highest grossing film in the US.

Meanwhile, on Lakertya …

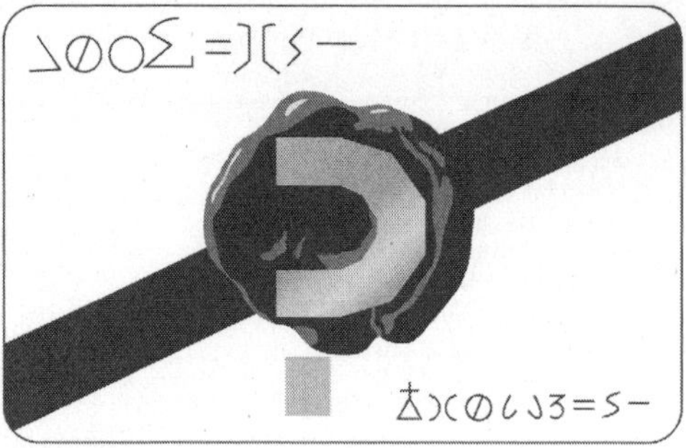

24a – *Time and the Rani*

> 'Time and tide melts the snowman'

The Rani forces the TARDIS off course in order to plonk the Doctor's brain inside her honking great brain so it can work out something or other to do with an asteroid and… dunno – blow up some Lakertyans?

Upside-down The Rani the right way up.

The Rani's Lair of Flair

'A Lakertyan; a race so indolent they can't even be bothered to bury their dead' says Rani-Mel staring at Farooooooooon's skeletal corpse in a moist quarry.

Let's consider this indolence. If the Lakertyans are so lazy, who built their Leisure 'Hive' and who built the Rani's lair?

One could assume for the sake of argument that the lair was a 'found' building, but it seems incredibly well-designed to house a brain, brain-juice pumping station and brain-feeding people-chambers, as well as a bat cave for the Tetraps to dangle in and drink Yazoo from a grimy gutter. So for the sake of argument, one would be wrong. If you thought that, you were wrong. You idiot.

It's clear that the lair was built to the Rani's specifications and it's a pretty big structure complete with the aforementioned luxuries, a red carpet entrance and a rocket launch pad with spinning satellite dish. So who built it? Was it the Tetraps? It seems unlikely. The Tetraps don't seem terribly practical and their eyes dart about like guilty pimps in a holding cell. The odds of them building something that doesn't look like a frightened tree are fairly remote. Mind you, the Rani can build her own frightened trees.

There's a thought – presumably that brain gunk she's been half-inching in *Mark of the Rani* is used to make the Lakertyans all lazy and stuff. But that doesn't make sense either, why would she *want* them to be lazy? She's got a honking great brain to build in order to blow up an asteroid in order to… well we forget the actual plan. But that's the least of our worries.

Let's accept that the Lakertyans were used as slave labour to build the Rani's lair, under the stewardship of the Tetraps led by Urak. In order to do this, every last detail will have been decided on by the Rani since Tetraps are clearly not big on interior design, carving our rock-faces etc. They basically hang upside down in caves all day. Speaking English. Or backwards-English if you read the book. Don't read the book, it's awful.

Urak, as Site Supervisor, must've been working from plans. Those plans would have either been commissioned or coerced from a responsible, capable architect (or, as this is a Pip and Jane script, let's say 'Space Architect'). I say 'coerced' because it seems unlikely the Rani, being an evil genius, would pay for such a service. But also I feel rather sorry for the architect who one day found himself set upon by a gang of Tetraps and forced to draw up plans for an evil, hollowed-out-cave lair. No doubt at gun-point.

> 'REKEELS STELIOT EHT EKAM!' snarled Urak, pushing the crappy plastic gun into the frightened architect's sweaty temple.

Of course the architect would still have to be working to the Rani's exacting needs and would doubtless have all manner of questions for her. This in turn presents a rather strange cross-interrogation:

RANI	Build me a fortress!
ARCHITECT	Certainly, Mistress Rani. What sort of fortress?
RANI	A magnificent fortress carved into the side of a quarry.
ARCHITECT	Okay. What will it be used for?
RANI	Trembling fool! Do you think I would divulge my fiendish plans to just anyone?
ARCHITECT	Well it would be helpful. I mean, do you

	need a kitchen?
RANI	Probably.
ARCHITECT	Gas or electric? In fact, how do you want the whole thing powered if it's in a quarry?
RANI	I don't know, a generator or something.
ARCHITECT	Solid fuel or liquid?
RANI	You decide.
ARCHITECT	How many bedrooms?
RANI	None. One. And a cave for the Tetraps.
ARCHITECT	Just one bedroom? Are you sure? What if you have guests?
RANI	Okay, two. Two and the cave.
ARCHITECT	Single or double beds?
RANI	Single.
ARCHITECT	I see.
RANI	What's that meant to mean?
ARCHITECT	Bathroom – will you have staff? Do you need male/female toilets?
RANI	Yes. No. Don't know. Later.
ARCHITECT	Windows?
RANI	No. None at all. But I'd like a little scanner screen in the central table.
ARCHITECT	Central table?
RANI	Yes. Square-ish. A couple of drawers. Wide enough for a shortish man to lay on.
ARCHITECT	What colour?
RANI	What are the options?
ARCHITECT	Well if you could let me know your budget, what materials will be available etc.
RANI	The local environment is rich in stone, slate and tinsel.
ARCHITECT	I can work with that.
RANI	I want a big flame-lit red carpet entrance too.
ARCHITECT	Won't the carpet get wet?
RANI	Whose lair is this?

ARCHITECT	Red carpet. Right. No problem. Anything else I should know?
RANI	I want a bloody great rocket launch pad on the roof.
ARCHITECT	The roof? Why not next to it? I mean a rocket taking off can be pretty hot.
RANI	*On the roof!*
ARCHITECT	It's just that the ceiling will need to be heavily reinforced and…
RANI	I said on the roof! With a little spinning satellite dish.
ARCHITECT	What's the dish for?
RANI	I don't know.

You see there's just so much she needs to make up her mind about and one assumes Lakertya is a pretty big planet. They must have local building regulations of some sort. Fire exits, disabled access, drainage. The despot lair is a very specific thing. Does the Rani have a chill-out room? Does she wind down at the end of the day on a big comfy sofa with a box set of **The Pallisers** or does she live for the work, day in day out? She certainly has to stop for dinner which is why the kitchen question came to mind. Being the Rani though she's probably developed some sort of 'nutrient pills' which, since this is a Pip and Jane script, are probably called 'Space Food'. Her disgust at the Lakertyan indolence however does imply that she's something of a workaholic.

Now we've got an architect who's responsible for the general space, but we still need all the mechanical gubbins and presumably an interior designer. Let's face it, the Rani's pad is pretty keenly decked out in eighties peach. Someone chose that colour, and she has form since her TARDIS in *Mark of the Rani* is a pretty sleek number. Speaking of her TARDIS, it would appear her chameleon circuit has gone fudgy since we last saw her since that big pink mirrored triangle doesn't really blend in with the grey, slate-covered environment it's in. As Terrance would say, it's incongruous. Except he'd probably say 'incongwoos'.

So interior design has been taken into account. This in itself is odd since she may as well have used the cave walls rather than plastering, painting and beautifying the environment. I suppose it's possible she needed to keep the environment sterile for the sake of her really big brain so for now we'll just have to accept that and move on to the more pressing issue of the rocket sled.

The 'Loyhargil' plan revolves around a well-timed rocket and since the Rani is chiefly a chemist, much as I'd like to believe she's clever enough to work all this out for herself, I doubt very much that she oversaw the construction of both the rocket *and* the launch pad. This again would've required a specialist in rocket technology and I strongly believe she would've outsourced this to a contractor. You don't want slave labour building such a key piece of equipment in your dastardly plan. They just can't be trusted. We've all purchased a pair of supermarket trousers, the zip can snap just like that. This is definitely an area where the Rani would've had to spend some money, or at least a deposit up front.

The problem now is that all this would've taken time. She didn't actually know where the rocket would need to be fired until the massive brain worked it out, so what if after building all this the brain said 'No, sorry. You missed your chance. We need to build a rocket sled on the next planet now.'?

You'll have to imagine that said in one of Peter Tuddenham's three voices.

Even if she gave herself a calculated margin of error, she still had to rely on those contractors to finish on time which is extremely unlikely. There would've been all sorts of issues and certainly at some point they'd have to do a test run of some sort.

Time and the Rani? Time and Money more like. There's just so much wrong with the Rani's plan and the key problem is that she seems to have expended far more energy and time on décor, design and red carpets than she ever did on… whatever the hell her plan was.

We Want Bwwwwaaaaiinnsss…

Aside from being a smart arse, just what exactly is the giant brain for? Yes, we know it's about a substance called Loyhargil, but what's that? How does tapping the brains of a bunch of nerds and feeding them into the ultimate brainiac produce something which can blow up an asteroid made up of strange matter? But when it does and she launches her missile at the asteroid full of the stuff, what then? Other than a sucking great hole in space/time right on her doorstep, what will it do? Is the Rani's plan for the pure glorification of science or is she planning on doing something else, assuming she's able to escape the event horizon/bloody enormous blast/sudden outpouring of strangeness. Oh, nothing so silly – she wants to create a time manipulator purely so that she can go back to Earth and allow the dinosaurs to survive. All that because she has a penchant for prehistoric monsters. You'd think the tyrannosaurus rex that grew in her TARDIS the last time she met the Doctor would cure her of that peccadillo. Besides, if that's all she really wanted to do, then there are far easier ways of ensuring dinosaurs survive: Perhaps generating them in a lab *like she did last time*. Seriously, what is it with this woman and big scaly monsters?

Should Have Gone to Specsavers

The truly remarkable thing about Tetraps is that they have four eyes with one on each side of their head, as opposed to us humans who, for the most part, only have two on the front. This advantage allows them to have incredible 360° vision which is a real boon for the professional hunter or savage. But just as we know from our own experiences, not everybody has perfect eyesight. Myopia would be a huge problem for a Tetrap as they are extremely reliant on their eyes. Just where would a Tetrap get some spectacles? It is clear from the desolate nature of Lakertya that shopping facilities are limited – there isn't even a branch of Lidl – so a Tetrap in need of a pair (we say 'pair', but the four-eye business means that they should probably really be called a 'set' as they'd have to be some sort of contraption that could fit right around the head) of glasses really would struggle to find an optician.

(If a branch of Vision Express existed on the planet, then 'Express' probably wouldn't be a suitable term due to the fact that four eyes would have to be examined for each patient, rather than two. When we went to get our eyes tested the other week it took long enough, as the optician was very thorough. He looked right into the eyes, did all of those tests with the letters and the red and green circles, he blew some air into the eyes to test the reflexes, and even took photographs to determine the well-being of the back of the eyes. Now, imagine an optician having to do that *four times* for each patient – it'd be a nightmare and would take *ages*. And Lakertyans are lazy. This would have the result of appointments taking much longer, there'd be fewer appointments per day and the waiting lists would be lengthier than any reasonable person would be prepared to tolerate. It would also cost twice as much and given Tetraps probably don't get paid very highly, you wonder if they would even bother spending *any* money on eye care. Life would be really tough for a Tetrap).

If a Tetrap had the nous then he could perhaps fashion himself some lenses from some pieces of discarded glass, but Tetraps don't really display that level of ophthalmological knowledge and such improvised glasses could be more of a hindrance. They can't even walk into glitter without getting confused. If our Tetrap – we'll call him Alan – were unable to get specs, then his life and wellbeing would be seriously compromised. Alan would most likely relegated to the runt of the pack and would probably be given the simple, menial tasks such as shifting rocks from one place to another that none of the others wanted to do. This would undoubtedly be a very worthless and degrading endeavour and it wouldn't be surprising if Alan turned to drink, possibly even losing his wife in the ensuing decline into depression. His wife is probably called Clair/Claire/Clare/Klair.

So before succumbing to depression, he'd want to seek professional help. To whom could he turn? There have been plenty of scientists in the world of **Doctor Who** but there aren't that many who have specialised in eye care. Mehendri Solon was a bit of a tinkerer with heads, but didn't have a great deal of success when it came to eyes. He created his hero with the best materials that he had available, but poor Morbius ended up with two plastic stalks for eyes and four of those just wouldn't look right on a Tetrap. Professor Rubeish, whom the Doctor encountered during *all that business* (phrase © Barry Letts/Jo Grant) with Linx the Sontaran, would be a much better choice as he conquered his own virtual blindness by discovering those extremely powerful spectacles. Whether he could apply his extensive knowledge of the subject of ophthalmology to those who have more than the usual pair of eyes though is debatable and we suspect that any optician dealing with a Tetrap would have a real problem with all of the hair.

If a particularly enterprising scientist did manage to crack the problem of Tetrap eye wear then he may well go on to market his new device on Lakertya and possibly even further afield if there were other alien races in need of such a product. The invention would therefore need a careful branding strategy applied to it and a name would need to be created for it. As we mentioned earlier 'spectacles' would be no good as they only apply to two-lensed optical aids, so something like 'Vision Halo', 'Quadragegs' or 'Crown of Sight' would be better to use in this instance. This inventor could make an absolute fortune, although we doubt that he or she would accept carrion from a Tetrap as a valid form of payment.

A dental surgery wouldn't go amiss on this planet either.

For more information on ophthalmology, why not read Michael Seely's *Quest for Pedler: The Life and s of Dr Kit Pedler* also available from Miwk Publishing.

Loyhargil

We're pretty clever here at Auton. We've noticed something you haven't, mainly because you're probably a bit thick. But we found out that 'loyhargil' is an anagram of 'Holy Grail'. Mind you, it's also an anagram of 'Golly Hair' so it's just as well Mr Ratcliffe isn't in this story.

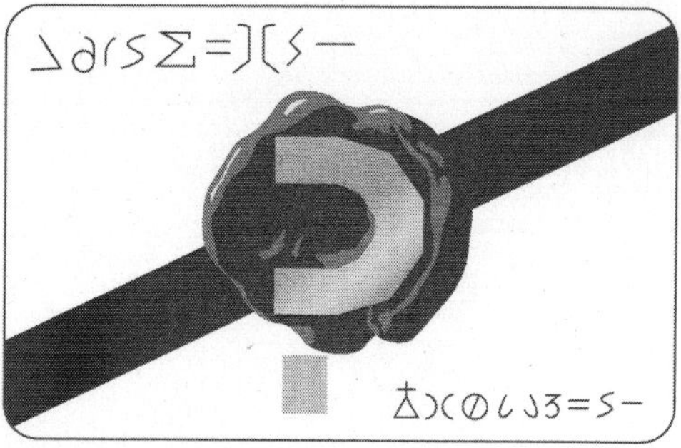

24b – *Paradise Towers*

'Mel, Mel! What a delicious name!'

In search of a swim, the Doctor and Mel arrive at Paradise Towers, a luxury block of flats built by the renowned architect Kroagnon. Alas, it's all gone a bit Croydon inside.

Tabby (or Tilda, I don't know which is which) eating Grey Kang*

* (we can't afford to print colour)

So Who's Best?

It's hard to quite know where to begin when it comes to the Kangs. On the one hand the prospect of gangs of teenage girls running about the place with wild abandon is, to be sure, a terrifying one. Just looking at any high street on a Friday night to confirm that much. Never underestimate the destructive power of a clutch of Bacardi Breezers in the wrong hands. But this lot seem mentally stunted; their playground jibes are seemingly innocent enough but those little crossbows they wave about didn't come from Claire's Accessories. They're properly dangerous. It's just that it's hard to really be worried by Kangs too much as they holler like kids, act like kids, dance about like kids and dress like kids. Clearly life in the miserable corridors of Paradise Towers has led to their desperate state, but they don't appear to be particularly violent, weapons and deaths aside. Rather, they seem to treat their existence as one long round of tag.

Mel gets the measure of the Kangs almost immediately – silly little girls who could really use a proper spanking and jolly well learn to grow up. That's why they don't want her to be a Kang. It's not like Mel to be quite so judgmental, but then again, she really does want to get to that pool before it closes.

Of course, the mystery of the Kangs is explained unwittingly by Fire Escape shortly after she meets the Doctor:

'Boys? What are boys?'

Although, given that there are men knocking about Paradise Towers, that's a surprising gap in Kang knowledge. Okay, so the caretakers aren't much to look at in their drab grey uniforms with their wide staring eyes, but there's always Pex. Innate cowardice aside, there's no denying he's beefy. Has sexuality been completely erased form the genetic make-up of Paradise Towers? Not if the clothes the Kangs wear are any indication. Let's face it, for all their torn, shabby appearance, those outfits highlight the female form in no uncertain terms. And on the other side of the sexy coin, Pex is clearly dressed to impress. But impress who?

The Kang Way

Just to elaborate a little further on the Kangs and their crossbows, what are the crossbows for? We're told that 'To make unalive is not the Kang way' and they brandish the crossbows defensively. If they don't want to kill, why the crossbows? It's difficult to do much else with a crossbow. Yes, you can shoot someone in an arm or a leg, or in the case of a Tetrap, the fourth eye ('He was shot right in the fourth eye, nasty way to go...') but there are no noticeable medical facilities in Paradise Towers so the wound is likely to get infected and the patient will bleed to death.

Where did those crossbows come from anyway? They've got hundreds of the things. The caretakers aren't armed, so why does a luxury building have such an excess stock of crossbows? Did someone get an order wrong? Maybe something called a 'cross bolt' is used for door mechanisms like the one that fails on the Doctor in the final episode?

Another possibility is that Paradise Towers has shops. More on that later.

Driller Killers

Kroagnon makes it very clear that the cleaning robots (herein referred to as Cleaners) are his. So he presumably designed them. Not just an architect, but also a closet **Robot Wars** fan.

Consider for a moment how you clean your kitchen, bathroom and house. Maybe you don't, maybe you sit in your own filth. But pretend you're that posh woman across the road for a moment and then consider how your local authority goes about cleaning the streets. Now ask yourself: which three tools could you not do without in your standard day-to-day cleaning? That's right: Saw blade, drill and grabbing claw.

Let's start with the drill. There's very little you can clean with a drill. We tried all this week on a variety of things from the car, the toilet, the windows and the cat. You can't clean any of those with a drill. You can however drill holes into them and effectively break them. But the holes are the easiest thing to achieve with the drill. *In theory* you could use the drill to break heavier, more cumbersome pieces of litter and detritus down into more manageable chunks. Perhaps the drills are just for maintenance? After all we've seen inside the Rezzie apartments, they all have pictures on the wall. Well no, the cleaners can't have done that because the drill is at a fixed level around shin-height and even then, the diameter of the drill is such that even at the finest point of the helix it's still a good inch across even at low-depth penetration. The hole would be almost as wide as the picture. This drill attachment is of no practical use on a cleaning robot (okay, from HERE it's referred to as a Cleaner).

This morning we attempted to clean a few things with a saw blade. This is trickier than the drill because the saw blade itself only really does anything when it's spinning. If you're prepared to hurt your gums you can at a pinch pick your teeth with it. You can also gently use it as a brush/comb for your hair. This in turn means it has grooming potential for a number of hirsute things such as cats, dogs, Rezzies, Kangs and ball sacks. Lunge at any of the above with a saw blade and they don't like it. So forget the grooming potential for now.

You can use the drill to make pretty patterns on carrots before you slice them, but this isn't technically 'cleaning'. You can also make those shitty swirls you see on Artex ceilings. Again, this isn't cleaning it's just 'spoiling plaster'.

Things you can't do with a saw blade:

> Remove build-up of leaves from a gutter
> Get bird poo off a car bonnet
> Remove dirt from a child's face
> Cleanse encrusted rear channel of lavatory bowl
> Pick grain of sand from eye
> Wipe bottom
> Wipe any other body part
> Sweep road/floor/cupboard tops

The best use for a saw blade is to saw something. This usually means taking, for example, a piece of wood, and bisecting it with a smooth, neat finish. This does not tally with any known usage of cleaning utensils.

Finally we have the grabber claw. This is easily the most practical of all the Cleaner's tools. It can reach out, pick something up, and deposit it in a handy rear-mounted trailer. Claw arms are commonly used for a variety of tasks, for example a litter picker in a park might use a long stick with a handle which, when squeezed, opens and closes a claw arm at the other end, saving them from leaning down to pick up rubbish or dog poo with their bare hands.

The major difference between the traditional cleaning claw attachment and the Cleaner claw attachment designed by the

Great Architect Kroagnon, is that the traditional claw *closes* completely forming a seal, thereby allowing it to pick something up, be it a crisp wrapper, a discarded biscuit (Bourbon, Jammie Dodger, Custard Cream), used condoms or a severed Kang leg. Therefore the attachment on the cleaning robot (from now on referred to as Cleaner) is relatively useless unless you take the claw in both hands and hold it to your throat (for examples, see Doctor and Tabby).

Attachments aside, the cleaner has a few other unusual features. One is an inability to see through thin lace tablecloths but this is more of a design flaw than a selling point. The cleaner can also spray a relatively harmless white mist from its mechanised udders and has an attractive 'flashing light' accessory.

When you look around a room, where does the dirt tend to build up? In the corners. I bet you read that before you thought of a better answer. You div. But here's the thing: Cleaners have a rounded base. This means it's physically impossible for them to get into corners. This is why Paradise Towers is so filthy and ramshackle. It's got nothing to do with the lake of care from the takers or the Kangs wallscrawl or the Rezzie's discarded bog roll – it's because the robots designed to execute a single function are ill-equipped to fulfil that simple function. Stoopid Kroagnon.

We all know that if you really want to get in corners, you need to be Sophie Aldred.

So, Again: Who's Best?

Where exactly do the Kangs come from? As the war was fought many years ago, these girls can't have been around at the time so they must be the descendants of the original residents of

Paradise Towers. Do their parents become Rezzies? The Rezzies are the only elderly people around the place, but from what we see they are old, possibly gay and therefore, within the Paradise Towers environment, less likely to have had children. The men have all been sent away to fight (apart from that weedy shit Pex), so where do the fathers of the Kangs come from? Are special bags of spunk brought in to fertilise the women of the tower, and if so who is organising all of this? How are the bags allocated? Is there some sort of raffle to see who gets which bag, is it just random or can the person pick which sample they want? Are the women provided with any details of who has provided the sample? To be honest, we are just speculating here but if fairly obvious plot strands aren't covered on screen then we have to make up our own answers to these unasked questions.

How is it that only girls appear to be born in the Towers, and if boys are born where have they gone? They can't all go on to become Caretakers because the Towers wouldn't require that level of staffing. If they are sent away to fight you have to think that it is rather cruel to put baby boys on the ships off the planet. They couldn't even fight properly at that age, as they wouldn't be able to hold a gun correctly. No wonder they're losing the war.

Ocimum Basilicum

If you were able to stop sniggering at the words 'mum' and 'cum' long enough then you'd remember that this is the Latin name for the herb basil. Basil's name stems from the Greek word for king: basileus. This is how highly regarded it is as a herb.

You, being the sort of trampy low-life you are, probably don't use herbs in your cooking except when you buy a Schwartz powder for your Bolognese (or as you call it: 'spag bol'), or when you're shaking sachet after sachet of salt over your fatty, chavvy chips in Wimpy or Burger King or something.

Some herbs are better when dried, but most are preferable when fresh. Basil should be used as fresh as possible, and if using it you wouldn't normally add it to anything until the last possible moment. For example try this: Slice several tomatoes in half, place a thin slice of garlic on each one, a drizzle of olive oil, salt and pepper (this is called *seasoning*). Whack 'em in the oven, around gas mark six, for twenty minutes. Take them out and tear some fresh basil onto them. Serve as a starter or side dish. Lovely. Because basil and tomatoes belong to each other.

Why the recipe? Well we cook. We're familiar with the tastes and flavour of each herb and what they're best served with. Basil is not a herb you would commonly use with meat. Melanie Bush is made from meat. If you cook Melanie Bush she would *not* be a vegetarian option. She is *at least* 90% meat, even though she probably only eats carrots and seeds.

So as Tilda skips across her front room announcing she'll fetch 'the basil' – what's it for? Are they knocking up a sauce maybe to cook Mel in? If so we don't believe basil would be a good match for Mel. If we were to eat Mel, and we're not saying we're going to, but if we were to eat her, we'd expect her cooked meat to taste not unlike lamb. We know they say (huh, what do *they* know?) that human meat tastes like chicken, but not Mel. She's definitely got a lamby thing about her. Maybe it's the curly hair? She does resemble a big shaggy ginger lamb. In truth, Bonnie Langford probably tastes of roses and toffee. She's just so damn adorable and sweet. But Mel is a character played by the actress Bonnie Langford and Tabby and Tilda, the Rezzies, are cooking Mel, not Bonnie. Mel tastes of lamb.

Lamb and tomatoes do go together, but not 'on the bone' as Tabby seems to like her Kang. Mel, much as she's lovely, doesn't have much meat on her and one imagines her 'rump' would be along the lines of a spare rib. It would require slow cooking to get the best out of it.

It's possible the Rezzies are prepping a side salad to go with Mel, but if they have these ingredients to spare, why bother with the meat course?

Actually, where does the fresh cream come from for their tea and cakes? They're very generous with it, offering Mel huge great dollops of their creamy white slop on her tiny sweet, sweet cookie. We have some theories:

1. It's some sort of long-life or frozen cream.
2. They milk each other.
3. They milk the rats.
4. Paradise Towers, like any other tower block, is in the middle of a town somewhere and they just nip out to the nearest shop like Londis or something.

They also have cakes and crumpets and a budgie they've not stooped to eating. But the cakes and crumpets again are either frozen or made by Tabby and Tilda (and the other Rezzies). We already know that 'most' of the Rezzies make tablecloths. This in itself is really weird! What are they doing with all those tablecloths? The answer is clear: Outside Paradise Towers they have a little stall set up where they swap tablecloths for flour, milk, eggs, yeast, cocoa powder, hundreds and thousands etc.

But for whatever reason, even with salad, herbs and a variety of cakes available to them, some of the Rezzies have taken to eating Yellow Kangs. In a 2001 study (going back a bit here) it was discovered that the popularity of Starbursts (formerly Opal

Fruits) went orange, yellow, green, red, purple while the popularity of Smarties (always Smarties) was orange, yellow, brown, red, purple. At this stage blue Smarties had yet to become a permanent fixture like the green and white Smarties or the tan/light brown ones which you'd only get in pick 'n' mix. But it shows that people, as Heston Blumentahl has often maintained, eat with their eyes. The Yellow Kangs, because of their unfortunate choice of gang colour, made themselves the tastiest to the Rezzies (and Cleaners alike).

Let us also ponder on the Rezzie technique of capturing their prey. They don't know who Mel is, and there are never any visitors (or ball games or out-going) to Paradise Towers so she's got to be a Kang. Kangs, as we've discovered early on, are a feisty bunch. They're not given to fanciful notions of 'feet up' and 'afternoon tea'. How odd then that Tilda adopts this method of capture with Mel? Are we to take it that the Yellow Kangs were all like Mel? Just happy to be spoken to, glad of the company, a little bit peckish for cream of dubious origin? Maybe the Yellow Kangs also clip-clopped up and down the corridors yelling 'Doctor!'? The truth is that the Blue and Red Kangs, although 'making unalive' is not the Kang way, have a habit of firing crossbow bolts at strangers. They're distrustful of Rezzies and know that Rezzies make Kangs unalive. So what the hell was Tilda playing at? 'Would you like a cup of tea?' – did the Yellow Kangs really fall for that? If so it serves them right that they got wiped out.

And are the Rezzies really going hungry? Tabby and Maddy are hardly svelte. If we assume Tilda is lactose intolerant, then maybe the Rezzie diet consists solely of cream of dubious origin (CODO) and their exercise regime is made up of crocheting tablecloths. This would explain their size. If food is so scarce, why would they need a full operable waste disposal? Surely every last scrap is important to them?

For the record: Yellow Kang herbs: Tarragon and garlic. Treat as chicken.

Red Kang herbs: Slow-cook with bay. Treat as beef.

Blue Kang herbs: Don't eat the blue ones.

Speak Kang:

How you do	Hello
Unalive	Dead
Carrydoors	Corridors
Wipeout	Killing Spree
Build High for Happiness	Hooray/Hello/Goodbye/I've got the horn
Ice Hot!	Fuck me!
Musclebrain	Idiot
Inbetweens	Adults
Oldsters	Old people
Brainquarters	Headquarters/base
Catch us if they can	Impregnate us

Rules are Rules

You would assume that a building the size of Paradise Towers would require a great many rules to keep it running smoothly. What the viewer sees of the place clearly indicates that it is in decline and is apparent that many, if not all, of the rules are no longer being adhered to. The Caretaker's Manual appears to be a rather flimsy green notebook (entitled simply 'Rules'), which seems insufficient considering the size of building it has to cover. It must only have around a hundred pages and surely cannot contain all of the instructions required to manage such a large estate. Is this tome merely a digest of the full manual, or is it something that the Chief Caretaker has just come up with off his own initiative? There must be a multi-volume longer version held somewhere. Fair enough, it has to be portable enough for the Caretakers to carry around with them, but you would have thought that a society that can come up with Paradise Towers would be able to come up with some sort of electronic version. We suspect that Kroagnon played no part in the formulation of the manual and most likely just lets the Chief Caretaker run things as he sees fit as long as it doesn't interfere with his ultimate plans.

Unseen Rules from the Caretaker's Manual

> No caretaker shall look at the human known as 'Pex'.
> No caretaker shall speak to the human known as 'Pex'.
> No caretaker shall acknowledge the existence of the human known as 'Pex' or engage with him in any way.
> No caretaker shall interfere with any Kang. Touching, fondling, licking, grabbing, shaving, fingering, tickling, bumming and speaking to them are ALL prohibited.
> No caretaker shall interfere with the human known as Pex. Touching, fondling, licking, grabbing, shaving,

fingering, tickling, bumming and speaking to him are ALL prohibited.

No caretaker shall carry out any maintenance on or on behalf of any Rezzie.

No caretaker shall carry out any maintenance on any Rezzie.

Any Caretaker caught pimping out Kangs shall be dismissed from his position immediately.

No Caretaker shall go anywhere near the Top Secret basement.

Selling the Dream

Golden Dream Park, The Bridge of Perpetual Motion, Miracle City are just a few of the other inventions of the Great Architect, but his crowning glory has to be Paradise Towers. It was originally intended to be a truly magnificent achievement where the rich and privileged could live, but we wonder how the owners managed to market it to the public. Kroagnon doesn't actually want anybody to live in the buildings that he designs, as he is a bit like one of those people who buy action figures and then don't play with them, but the investors would surely want to get some return on the money that they had put into the scheme. We get to see a brief glimpse of the blueprints for the building during the story that clearly states that the basement is out of bounds 'On pain of death'. If you had the money and were considering purchasing an apartment here, would this fact not raise an alarm with your surveyor? Homes have been rejected by purchasers for much more trivial matters than this, so it is incredible that the Towers ever gained any residents. Any sensible surveyor would query the 'pain of death' aspect of the building.

Who's Breeding all the Budgies?

Tabby and Tilda have a budgie. It's clearly a budgie and it sounds like a budgie. Let's be clear on this: it could be a Space Budgie.

Budgies live for 8 years, sometimes 10 if they're lucky, but the average life expectancy is 8 years. We've already established that food is scarce in Paradise Towers so bird seed is presumably not an option. Budgies don't eat meat (nor do Space Budgies, we checked with a Space Vet). So this is unlikely to be a particularly well-fed budgie. Let's therefore give it a life expectancy of 5 years, and that's being generous.

This 'Great War' is implied to have happened within living memory, but so long ago that everyone's forgotten. Well someone would remember better details of a war five years ago, so this budgie can't be the one Tabby and Tilda started with can it? This means someone in Paradise Towers is breeding budgies. Not only that, but someone in Paradise Towers has a heck of a lot of bird seed handy. Maybe bird seed is used as currency?

Budgies are pretty noisy, and surely Paradise Towers has a 'no pets' rule?

Is it possible that Kroagnon could've transplanted his brain into the budgie if he'd had the chance? That would've been really cool.

'How-you-do? I'm Bog Brush'

How do the Kangs get named? Are they nicknames or birth names? Are their real names things like Patricia, Leslie and Aoife? If they are nicknames, how do they acquire them?

Bin Liner: This is either in reference to her being good at cleaning (unlikely, the Towers are messy) or full of rubbish. We'll go for the latter.

Fire Escape: Our best bet is a windy bottom problem.

Air Duct: Presumably the same reason that girl I knew from Essex was known as 'the Bucket'

Drinking Fountain: We're just going to stop here. This gets really filthy…

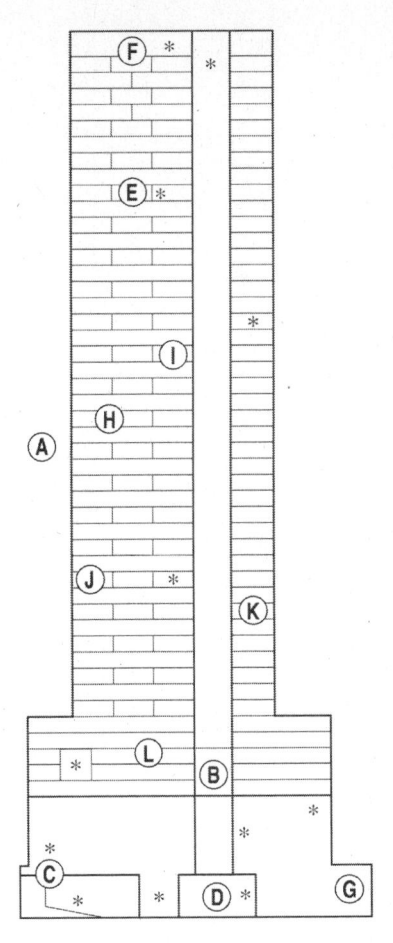

Map showing grounds and environs of Paradise Towers
A—Tower B—Entrance C—Stairs to Secret Basement
D—Secret Basement E—Tabby & Tilda F—Swimming Pool
G—Red Kangs H—Yellow Kangs I—Blue Kangs
J—Green Kangs K—Pex L—Caretakers
*—Potential Area of Death

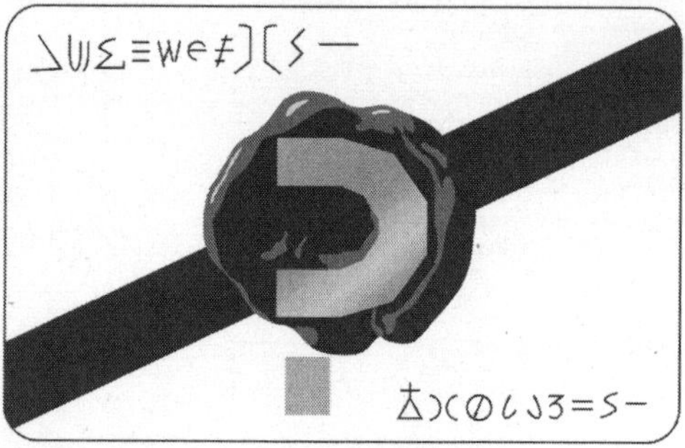

24c – *Delta and the Bannermen*

> 'I shall ask my bees ...'

Having crash-landed at a Butlins camp in Wales, Mel and some aliens become embroiled in the machinations of an intergalactic exterminator named Gavrok.

Egg (holed) and the Bannermen.

Mel's Surprisingly Capacious Bag

If you're going to spend a week, a whole week, in Disney Land, planet Earth, then you should certainly pack for the occasion.

In the history of **Doctor Who** we can't think of a single occasion when a companion packed extra clothes for their trip. We know the TARDIS has a wardrobe which if *Twin Dilemma* or *Time and the Rani* are anything to go by consists of seven or eight pieces of shit and one extremely tailored outfit perfectly suited to the person browsing therein.

Mel is not your typical companion. She knows that she and the Doctor have won a prize (she's never won anything before) and she's packed for a week, a whole week, in a very small suitcase. This isn't unusual in itself since Mel is remarkably petite and most of her clothes you could fit in your pocket or ear. We know we did when we raided her knicker drawer at the Yvonne Arnauld Theatre last Christmas.

The problem is, while Mel planned ahead, she never could've guessed she'd get through five outfits in the first night. Don't believe us? We arrive at Toll Port G715 and Mel is wearing a blue and white striped skirt with a white blouse and black jacket. She's also wearing some flat, sensible shoes.

Once they've arrived at Shanrgi La she finds out to her screaming excitement that there's going to be a 'Getting to Know You' dance that very night. Wonderful! How lucky that she's packed a dancing dress, a peach off-the-shoulder number. Look, there she is dancing with Murray the coach driver who only bought one outfit, just like every other person in the Navarino party. This makes sense because when they went through the transformation gate they were big naked purple bollocks, when they came out, they were clothed. It does seem a bit weird that they then took presumably empty suitcases with them. In fact a few of them take their jackets off during the dance so does that mean they're ripping off their own transformed flesh? Nasty!

So after a heavy night of dancing during which Billy makes eyes at Delta and sings her a lovely song that Ray wanted sung to her and didn't get so instead she spends the night on the laundry room floor with the dirty, dirty Doctor, Mel goes back to her room.

As she gets ready for bed in her full set of pyjamas which is essentially a track suit (and quite bulky to pack) Delta gets a bit more chatty and acknowledges just how nice Mel is. 'Thank you' she says, 'Thank you for being kind' isn't that nice? '…and lending me your dress' – what?! That's *also* Mel's dress? But Delta's a foot taller than Mel. And the dress is voluminous in the extreme. How did it fit in that tiny suitcase with the peach number and the pyjamas? *And* the denim suit with big red boots Mel's wearing the next morning? Yes, that's *another* outfit.

The biggest tragedy is that after all this, Mel leaves her magic suitcase and all those dresses behind. Unless she packed and dropped them off to the TARDIS before they left? After all, Delta doesn't keep the dress and instead prefers her Chimeron onesie. As does Billy. Where does Billy's onesie come from? Seems a strange thing to find on a Bannerman ship doesn't it? Maybe he grew it from drinking Delta's juice? After all, Delta's kid has one too and hers grew (along with the monster of all camel toes) as she screamed at some Bannermen hiding behind a pile of hay.

Where does Ray live? First thing in the morning she wakes up with the Doctor in her party frock but minutes later she accompanies the Doctor to warn 'old man Burton' about the

Bannerman war fleet. When did she get changed and why did she have the same clothes she was wearing yesterday so close to the holiday camp? It's not been established that she works there, just that she grew up near there. Why is Ray allowed to roam free in a holiday camp with a huge spiky metal fence that clearly takes security very seriously? She must stink of old knickers. Like our car boot.

Goronwy's Origins

Goronwy's the Doctor, isn't he, boyo? He's a future incarnation of Doctor Who, retiring to keep his bees in Wales. You might remember that in the Sherlock Holmes stories of Conan Doyle, one of the latest-set adventures, *The Lion's Mane*, concerns Mr Holmes in his retirement, keeping bees in Sussex in order to research his honey-nut cornflake idea. The Doctor has been identified with Sherlock Holmes a number of times – most notably in *The Talons of Weng-Chiang* – and so the sight of an elderly Time-Lord-ish gentleman pursuing a life as a beekeeper must be an obvious conceit for an ageing Doctor to take up. It's far too culturally relevant for him to miss the point, and we've come to the conclusion that Goronwy's living out his retirement in this way as a bit of a laugh about expectations. He's clearly the 43rd Doctor or whatever, having moved to Wales following his sacking from the position of Curator of the National Gallery as a result of his penchant for nipping back in time and writing 'this is a fake' under dozens of famous masterpieces. The events of *The Stolen Earth* also imply a deeper connection to intelligent bees, which have a measure of sentience (and they do call out to Delta in this story). Moreover, Delta hands Goronwy a green alien baby at one point, and the Welshish Time Lord doesn't bat an eyelid: obviously a consequence of the Doctor's in-built love of lime-flavoured jelly babies.

If this all sounds like a load of rancid old rarebit, then it's because we've just made it up. And yet the clues are there: the Cartmel stories contain several themes which support the assertion indirectly. *Battlefield* also deals with a future Doctor (Goronwy is Merlin!), *Ghost Light* mentions Conan Doyle, and bees are clearly behind the entire plot of *The Curse of Fenric* (actually, we've no evidence to support this one, but Fenric doesn't seem clever enough to have arranged it on his own if he can't finish off a simple game of chess).

The Bannermen and Vexilloligous Trifles

We're in the land of the literal when it comes to the Bannermen: they wear flags on their backs, hence the name. They're also mercenaries. So, what colours do the Bannermen wear and why? There's no sponsor evident in this adventure, and it appears that the wiping out of the Chimeron race and Delta in particular is a personal grudge on Gavrok's part. So the Bannermen are wearing their default colours of black and red.

But of course, the bane of the Bannermen is their very brand. They have to wear banners, otherwise they'd just be Men, or at a pinch, Horrible Men with Big Guns. We know they're mercenaries so presumably the colours they wear are those belonging to whoever has hired them. Which opens up a number of considerations:

1. They are useless for any job requiring stealth. Even wearing their default black and red they're easy to spot, thanks to those banners.

2. Who pays for the new colours every time they accept

a commission? Are new uniforms and banners part of the fee?

3. Such accessories cannot possibly be available off the peg, so somewhere out there is a Bannerman tailor and haberdashery department, whose sole task it is to knock up outfits in whatever style is required.

4. The wind. Wind is, of course, as much a part of a flag as the woven or man-made material itself. Without wind, a flag or banner is just a piece of cloth. The wind brings it to life, casting fear into the heart of the bearer's enemies, or pride into those over whom the flag flies. But to the one bearing a flag or banner, the wind can be as much an enemy as an ally. It's wonderful to have one's standard flapping proudly in the air, but when it comes to moving about, the fact that you're effectively carrying a sail on your back means that the wind has about as much control over where you're going as you do. Consider that when you look at the Bannermen atop that cliff edge. One strong gust and they'd be over.

So with all that in mind, just why do the Bannermen insist on being so? There can't be too much in the way of competition in the world of mercenary action, at least not out in public. Your mercenary is very much a creature of the underworld – they go in, get the job done, and they're out again. Results matter, reputation is king and one would assume corporate branding just isn't a major consideration. The sort of people who need a mercenary are usually the same sort of people who know where mercenaries can be found.

To our mind, Gavrok has severely misjudged his target audience with the whole concept of branding his gang. The initial idea of hiring "Bannermen" may sound attractive – it's a catchy name with historical undertones – the bannerman in battle being the one who let the enemy know you were coming. But the reality is not a crack troupe of badass military experts steeped in the lore of battle but a bunch of sunglass-wearing fashionistas with a penchant for theatricals. They may snarl convincingly (not necessarily in the story), but based on the evidence of Operation Bumblebee, or whatever they call it, they don't come with an impeccable track record. Even Gavrok, the hardest of the bunch, can't resist a little dig at the Doctor's white flag, claiming it "puny" in comparison to his lovely black and red zig-zagged number. He's a heady combination of Genghis Khan and Gok Wan.

This all presumes that the Bannermen were named prior to choosing the design for their outfits. It may be that they acquired the name Bannermen by reputation, a sort of slang term. It had never occurred to them that their banners were so unique.

Similarly, many planets hold records of The Big Collar Time Guys, Leatherbound Eggheads, and Judo Chop Green Spaghetti Monoid Splinter-Buggers.

Delta

Delta goes to great lengths to escape Gavrok and his band of banner-wearing, pink-gobbed idiots, but she's clearly no expert when it comes to going on the run. The first words out of her lips when she has supposedly reached salvation are 'No, I'm a Chimeron'. Fair enough, she wasn't to know there was a bounty hunter going on his holidays on the coach trip she sought sanctuary aboard, but you would expect a little more candour when barging your way onto a bus full of complete strangers.

It's not quite clear why Delta works so hard to blend in with her

fellow adopted travellers, when she's not prepared to go all the way. She turns up at breakfast wearing the same jumpsuit from her initial escape from Gavrok. Of course, as discussed, by the time of the "get to know you" dance she's found herself a rather fetching dress, courtesy of Mel and managed to stretch it out so that it fits her substantially larger frame quite beautifully. Not only that, she's also been giving Billy the glad-eye.
She's clearly new at the whole being a fugitive thing and unless she gets help soon is likely to go the way of the rest of her species. They're a Darwinian's dream come true, this lot. Presumably Chimeron the universe over where slaughtered at parties, dances, socials and happy hours while screaming 'I'm a Chimeron' at the top of their lungs.

The Joy of Eggs

The Chimeron reproductive system seems rather complex to human eyes and needs to be examined more closely. We've pondered deeply on this subject and need to know if Delta gives birth to a live baby out of her clacker like a human lady or not. If not, we wonder just how the egg comes out? Does she lay it chicken-style or is a caesarean section-type affair required? Does she *even have* the same parts like a human lady, or some sort of cloaca like a reptile or bird? Would the latter require a special sort of underwear to accommodate it, and can such a garment be obtained on Earth? If it can't then she wears the same knickers for the entire duration of this adventure. If she is physically like a human, then just how big is the egg when it is laid? Bigger than a human baby's head? From experience we know that giving birth looks as if it can be quite hard work. For all we know this is just silly women making a lot of fuss. Perhaps a more sensible explanation for giving birth to an egg would be if it started out quite small – perhaps the size of a Kinder Egg – and then grew larger once it was out. Another thing to consider about this egg is that it is all knobbly and spiny. Whichever way it exits the body it has to bloody hurt and we bet that some of the silver paint comes off too.

Of course we don't even know for sure that it's even Delta that laid the egg. It's given to her by the green bloke from the quarry/Alien Planet. Maybe among the Chimerons the boys do the egg-laying? Billy's in for a treat.

Care of the egg would be the top priority for Delta. A human baby is put into a cot to lie down after it has been born, but what the hell would a Chimeron on the run do with an egg? We see the egg in some sort of incubator device for a while but this device may not work properly on Earth. Does Delta instead have to build a nest in order for the egg to be safely incubated, and if so is the nest in a tree or on the ground? Would she have to sit on the egg as a chicken or ostrich does? We wonder if back on the Chimeron planet collectors illegally go after Chimeron eggs to display in cases in their sock drawers? Is egg theft on the Chimeron home planet a big problem? It could be considered a form of infanticide.

Let's say that Delta does need to build a nest for her egg. How exactly would she go about this in a crowded holiday camp full of holidaymakers? Would the nest need to be constructed with twigs and housed up a tree in the manner of a nesting bird would, or would she need to take the ground-nesting approach of the grouse and create a simple scrape nest on some waste ground? Whichever method she chooses the nest would need to be concealed from both holidaymakers and the camp staff. It would also have to be much larger than the nest of any Earth creatures and the holiday camp looks a very busy environment in which to host it. Due to the nest's size, somebody would most likely find it and smash the egg with sticks. The best approach would probably be for Delta to create the nest around the back somewhere near the bins and hope for the best. It really is bad luck that she found herself in Shangri-La and her situation would have been much better had the Nostalgia Tours coach crash-landed in a more remote environment such as on an uninhabited South Sea island or in a desert. Both she and her egg child would have been much safer.

Over the course of this adventure, we see that Billy becomes extremely enamoured with Delta. True, she is a decent looking woman and most men would probably be attracted to her, but for Billy she just has that something extra. We have to wonder if Billy was attracted to Delta purely on her looks, or did he somehow have an inkling that she may have been an alien queen decked out with a cloaca? Was Billy a cloaca fetishist in the first place who found that his luck was in when he discovered a beautiful woman replete with one, rather than him having to seek out wildfowl to satisfy his sordid cravings? In Delta he has the best of both worlds, quite literally. It's a great shame that we don't get to see the outcome of their pairing, as it would be fascinating to observe purely from a scientific view.

The baby Chimeron's head looks bigger than the egg itself. It must expand. It's an ugly little sod too. Why doesn't Billy flee when he sees it? Instead, he abducts Delta and the baby on his motorbike. The rapid-growth rate of the baby must be of interest to Billy as well. See the look in his eyes when he says: 'will she grow up to be a princess too?' He has a mad staring appearance that doesn't bode well. Just what are his intentions towards this child?

Further pondering on this matter makes us wonder what Billy would have experienced once he began his transformation into a Chimeron. Do all of his bits stay the same, or does he get a ghastly scaly, lizard part instead of his own gentleman's-sausage? Could he, you know, 'do it' with Delta prior to his transformation or would such an attempt result in a hideous, bloody mess with bits snapped off everywhere? Scientifically, we need to know if the component parts are compatible or not. Chimeron food may not even work on humans – after we leave them Billy might be transformed into something even more hideous than Delta's ugly baby. Like so much of **Doctor Who**, little is made clear resulting in confusion and disturbance in the mind of the viewer.

The Chimeron life cycle appears to be partly modelled on that of the Earth bee and this raises the question of whether Delta and Billy would live in a house or a hive once they get back to the Chimeron home world. Or indeed if they spend winter crawling around lethargically by patio doors.

Despite their newfound happiness, the pair have a huge task ahead of them in order to rebuild the entire Chimeron species. If there are only the two of them to do this then it raises the ugly problem of interspecies incest. If they can find more Chimerons then fine, if they don't then the Chimeron race could be in all kinds of genetic trouble which would rather render the entire preceding events something of a waste of time.

Hawk and Weismuller

Why does the FBI employ such a pair of bungling old fools? They clearly aren't up to the job due to their age. Sending this pair is like sending **The Golden Girls** to hunt down Osama Bin Laden. Whilst we should congratulate their employers for embracing people of all ages, perhaps their talents may have been working in a simpler area like Stores, a bit like old folk in this country do in B&Q.

We have to wonder what kind of work they did when they were

at the peak of their careers. Were they some of the big hitters who were active during important world events like the Second World War, or were they just stuck back in the post room at FBI HQ? Clearly they must have had something about them or they wouldn't have been dispatched to Wales on such an important mission to deal with a missing satellite, but from what Weismuller says to his colleague it seems that they already have something of a reputation for 'fouling up'. They've been sent to track a satellite but Jerome P. Weismuller says that he has never seen one before. You would have thought that he might, as a US government employee, have seen one in a book or something. And what about their boss? Did he or she not think to give them a photo of the bloody thing? We know from what Weismuller says that when he was an Eagle Scout and that he was good at knots, but is this his unique skill? Would this qualify for entry into the US secret service?

So, they've been sent to Wales without any specific instructions. Were they told to just wait there for orders? They look rather conspicuous to be undercover: Weismuller is dressed in baseball get-up (a good disguise for 1959 Wales), whilst Hawk is decked out in some sort of colonial style outfit. We like how they can get through to White House simply by going into a public call box and asking for the White House. Would they not have had to phone FBI HQ in Washington? Or does a Priority Call: Code (made on a public call box) somehow over ride normal operational procedures? We'd like to see who is on the other end of the phone as we bet that their boss is banging his head on the desk.

Nothing seems very urgent to them, despite their important mission. You would assume that their government would put them up in a hotel near Shangri-La somewhere, but they appear to be happy in their tent. They cook sausages on an open fire and have a nice picnic basket. They've just gone camping haven't they? We see that they are very interested in the wildlife of the area too as Weismuller tells the Doctor that they 'haven't even seen a squarrel this morning'. We aren't sure what a 'squarrel' is, but the correct American term for 'squirrel' is 'sqwirl'.

Their listening equipment is extremely rudimentary for tracking a satellite and they don't actually manage to find it themselves in the end. Hawk seems to be marginally more sensible of the pair but he just lets his colleague do more or less what he wants.

We'd really like to see the report that they had to file when they returned to America.

More than that, how did Gilmore and his rabble get a Big Finish spin-off and these two, nothing?

24d – *Dragonfire*

'Gordon Bennett, what a bunch of spots.'

The manager of a freezer centre hatches an elaborate plan to reduce his electricity bill and go home.

Kane I draw a map? Of course I Kane.

Maps, Heliophobia and Kane's Procrastination

Kane is a criminal, a warlord and a tyrant. Let us consider the punishment that the people of Proamon inflict on him.

They *could* sentence him to death, but that doesn't necessarily work, eye for an eye and all that. Or they could pop him in prison like Morgaine or the Master. Prisons don't often work due to the fact that people escape from them. Before we go any further we need to clear up a detail: How cold was Kane before his exile? Is Proamon a world of ice? Are the people of Proamon all dependent on the cold to live? If so, then we can proceed without issue. If not – has Kane become an icy lunatic during his exile? He's been there for three thousand years so it's possible. How is Iceworld powered? It can't even use solar energy and the main energy source for the whole place is inside a dragon's head.

Anyway, let us assume that Kane was icy to begin with because otherwise his army of frozen mercenaries don't make a lot of sense. If they're frozen, just like Kane, why doesn't he walk around with arms outstretched, each footstep accompanied by a synth stab? Why are the lower chambers of Iceworld warmer than those above? Doesn't heat rise? They must be, or Kane would live down below which would surely be more practical than sitting in a freezer for half the day. Without so much as a mattress.

Hey, if this is the DARK SIDE of the planet? Where does that sunlight come from at the end?

Anyway, Kane's prison could've just been a freezer surrounded by radiators and halogen spots. Presumably the people of Proamon wanted to humiliate him in his exile so was Iceworld, the ship, designed as a huge freezer centre or did Kane start that business? If so how did he go about it? Was he exiled with a massive pot of cash? No, it must've been a freezer centre and his humiliating exile was to be the manager of this freezer centre for eternity.

By the way, that Iceworld ship is *enormous*. It's wider than Europe if you assume Svartos is the same size as Earth. That's a huge freezer centre. Isn't that a bit wasteful for one pesky criminal?

Anyway, for three thousand years Kane had the opportunity to grab the Dragonfire and bugger off. Let's consider the evolution of Earth in three thousand years. Surely that pre-dates fire? So much has been achieved by the human race (not all of it stuff to be proud of: class system, rape, pollution, Jim Davidson) in that exceptionally long time. In our lifetime alone we've seen the evolution from the BBC Acorn through to the monster PC we're typing this on now. That's just a tiny aspect of technology. But Kane hasn't even mastered the glass-top freezer, something Iceland discovered back when it was a mere slip of a Bejam. He's still using those shitty old wire shopping baskets that were phased out years ago and replaced with rigid plastic ones. His signage is done on a bleeding Letraset!

But, when all is said and done, Kane applied himself. He made a go of Iceworld and it certainly seems to draw the punters in their dozens. It has a milkshake bar which is more successful than the frozen fish section, and dedicated senior management team capable of hunting ants with bazooka. Bazookas? What's the plural of bazooka? We want to say bazuki but we're fairly sure that's a musical instrument. Seems an odd thing to kill an ant with, but then pretty much anything will kill an ant, even Georgian folk music.

Kane is one of those rare things: An evil genius with a legitimate business front. For three thousand years he's cornered the market on frozen goods and seemingly let slip the notion of escaping. It's taken him three thousand years to get around to commissioning a sculpture of his dead girlfriend. What was that guy working from? There's no photo in evidence and I can't remember the faces of people I went to school with so how could he accurately describe his wife based on a three thousand year old memory? Actually that might explain why the statue is so shit. That sculptor got away with murder. Well he didn't, Kane squeezed his cheeks to death. We see Kane's missus in the Singing Gardens and she doesn't look a bit like the worn out ice-dildo that old guy knocked up.

Three thousand years. He's done *nothing* for three thousand years. All his efforts are focussed on the week before and during the Doctor and Mel's arrival.

Speaking of which – what was the tracking signal the Doctor had been picking up for some time? Is it the one in Glitz's map? Because that map's a bit confusing. Did Kane *make* the map, or is it a map he was given when he was exiled? Which silly sod thought it was a good idea to exile him with an instruction sheet on how to escape? Maybe they just thought it didn't matter since he's so bloody dumb he doesn't think to escape for three thousand years.

If the map was made merely to lure Glitz to the lower levels, why not send someone a bit more capable like Belazs? Glitz probably could've pulled it off if we're talking *Mysterious Planet* Glitz, but this is Pip and Jane Glitz. Pip and Jane Glitz is a bumbling comedy idiot. No, Belazs could've tracked down that dragon without any trouble at all. She has fire in her belly. Kane likes that. Which is odd given how hot fire usually is.

If Kane did make the map, he really went to a lot of trouble with it. It's a great piece of work. Does this mean he named the 'Singing Trees' and 'Ice Gardens'? Doesn't seem his style does it? Surely he'd have called them 'Death Howlers' and 'Place of Terror'? That he didn't shows a much keener, more romantic eye than the one that commissioned that bloody awful statue.

So we know Kane has had a map, three thousand years and an 'army' of frozen mercenaries he's been building up over those three thousand years. Even if we assume he's really shit at this and only manages to freeze one mercenary each year, that's still *three thousand* mercenaries *at least* that he could've sent en masse to capture the head of one very slow-moving, top heavy dragon.

Kane missed his calling. He's a lousy criminal but a damned savvy retail manager. His skill set is such that retail management is really his forte. Recruitment isn't his thing, his employee retention programme is a little heavy-handed, but generally speaking his staff seem fairly loyal and motivated which is more than can be said for your local branch of Iceland.

The Dragon

Looking back through history, tales of dragons abound. Fierce, horrible things with scaly bodies, dirty great teeth (usually dirty through all the maidens they've eaten) and all that fiery breath. The dragon on (or rather, in) Iceworld is most definitely at the lower end of the 'sorry, fair maid, you're on your own' scale. In fact, it's rather a graceful looking thing – like a ballet dancer with a giant cockroach balanced on its head. The frickin' laser beams are cool though.

As a protector of Svartos' most valuable treasure, it leaves rather a lot to be desired. The Doctor and his crew appear to be the first people to have come along in ages and rather than fry them with his laser eyes like he's programmed to, he gives them the full guided tour of his fortress of solitude then breaks his own skull in two to hand over the very thing he's supposed to be protecting. Again, Kane could have sent anyone down there with a friendly smile and they'd have been up and out of there before tea time. We increasingly have to come to the conclusion that Kane's decision to face the sun at the end of the story is purely out of shame at realising he's been such an unutterable moron for all those years.

There's also the question of why Kane's overlords would entrust their treasure to a fire-breathing dragon that lives in a network of ice caves. He's not really going to be able to use his lasers very much for fear of bringing the whole place down on top of himself. By this point we can't ignore the very real possibility that Kane was perhaps the least moronic of an ancient and venerable race of clueless idiots. That vengeance he keeps going on about, had he not dithered about for so bloody long, would have probably never come to pass anyway as the Proamons have probably have all died out by then anyway through sheer clumsiness or forgetting to breathe.

Sadly for the dragon, the Proamons instilled their own lack of sense into their most deadly of creations. Faced with a little girl lost in the ice tunnels, the dragon breaks cover and kindly escorts her back to the café. Good job no other poppets wandered down there in the preceding years or Kane and his mob would have had his head off in no time. The whole point of the creature was that he should remain hidden from Kane's icy grasp, not pop upstairs whenever he fancied a strawberry Krusha.

Glitz, Mel and a Lot of Frozen Mercenaries

The story continues, all stories do. The Doctor (ACE!) takes Ace (ACE!) away with him (ACE!) in the TARDIS (ACE!) leaving Mel (DOUGHNUT!) and Glitz (BIRDBATH!) behind (ACE!).

But they're not alone are they? There's still the kid and her mum and, as detailed earlier, a bare minimum of three thousand frozen mercenaries on that flying Bejam thing.

We've already established that it's a very large ship/shop. It's considerably larger than Europe, Asia and Africa combined. Glitz and Mel have only seen the equivalent of say, Regent's Park. It's really, really big. Presumably Iceworld itself makes up a very small part of the ship, now named *Nosferatu II*, with the rest given over to over stock and frozen mercenaries.

What's the plan for Glitz and Mel? A ship that size surely needs a crew? It's not been flown for three thousand years so must be in pretty poor condition. Also it appears to be powered by a small crystal, like running your whole house from an AAA battery. How long does the crystal last? It's been sitting in a dragon's brain for three thousand years.

Mel, at least, is an expert in computers. We've ascertained this much in our opening chapter. Actually, that's pretty much all Mel is. But at least she knows how to work the computer-side of things, even if it is technology three thousand years old. Glitz hasn't shown any ability as a pilot. The kid's mum, we need a name for her don't we? Let's call her Shriekhag Milkshakehead. Shriekhag could potentially be skilled as a pilot. She seems a bit posh and high-maintenance though which makes you wonder why she's slumming it in Space Bejam. There's not much in her carrier bag so presumably she's only bought a dozen prawns and a bit of cod. Seems a lot of effort to go to for such a small amount of shopping doesn't it? Docking procedures, walking around endless freezers with no way of knowing what's inside each one? We can of course assume from this that she's got other reasons for visiting Iceworld. We like to think she's the sculptor's wife killing time while he knocks out a quick ice statue for the general manager of the shop.

Finally, does Glitz speak English? Mel has been dumped on the middle of nowhere and without the Doctor or the TARDIS her ability to understand alien languages is no longer there. The signage in Iceworld was in English, but it's always possible that that's a translated version. That doesn't tally however with *The Curse of Fenric* where Ace can't read Russian. Mind you, it doesn't tally with *Delta and the Bannermen* either where Welsh isn't translated. It's like they're making it up as they go along. The writers that is, not the Welsh. Although…

The Danger of Dry Ice

We know it's called Iceworld and we know that Kane is the head honcho. We also know that Kane needs to be kept at a constant temperature significantly below our own human 37°C. So, Iceworld, or at least the secret parts of it behind the supermarket, like the stock room, manager's office, staff room and torture chambers, need to be kept cold to keep the boss happy. But why the dry ice? You don't get dry ice in cold rooms as a rule of thumb, just ice and cold air.

It's an affectation, isn't it? Kane likes to stride about the place being In Command and leaving a swirling trail of vapour in his wake. It's all about image with Kane; the white suits, the pointy hats, the pristine cleanliness and a knee-level cloud to really drive home the point that it's his base, it's cold and don't you forget it.

That cloud is, however, a health and safety nightmare. Nobody can see what's on the floor, where staircases end, where the bodies of discarded sculptors lie, waiting to be cleaned up. Kane's gang must spend half their time shuffling cautiously around the place for fear of tripping over a hidden obstacle or surprise bit of split-level flooring. Running is clearly out of the question, except in extreme situations, and even then the sickbay is full of them at the end of the day getting their broken toes and bruise shins tended to. Not to mention the fact that there must be absolutely no pets allowed. Not that they look the animal-loving type, but Kane's look would have been really enhanced by a white longhaired cat for him to stroke as he eulogises about how he's going to one day be free and all that guff he's so obsessed with. That said, one of the lizardy things in the milkshake bar has a pet thingy. It might not be a pet. It might be a dog-arm or something. We can only guess.

Kane's Birthday

Given that he has apparently been held prisoner on Svartos for millennia, where exactly does Kane keep all of his birthday presents? And just how old is he anyway? We know that things last longer if you keep them in a freezer, but surely even he has some sort of Best Before date? Fish Fingers don't even keep forever (We know, we tried). An intergalactic war criminal must be quite tricky to buy for and after so many birthdays there surely can't be much that Kane wants. There's only so many ice picks that he would want and a cake with a file in it would just risk irking him. We've come up with a list of presents for season 24 bad guys:

The Rani: Make up
Kroagnon: Dildo
Gavrok: Pork
Kane: Ferrero Rocher

Season 25

It all continued in 1988.

Kuwait Airways Flight 422 is hijacked, The Liberal Democrat party is formed, Celine Dion wins the Eurovision Song Contest, Windows 2.1 is released, Al Qaeda is formed, Phillip Morris buys Kraft Foods for $13.1bn, delaying his search for missing episodes, Rihanna, Haley Joel Osment and Rupert Grint are born, John Holmes, Kenneth Williams and Charles Hawtrey pass away (not in the same room) and **Rain Man** is the highest grossing film in the US.

Meanwhile, in Shoreditch ...

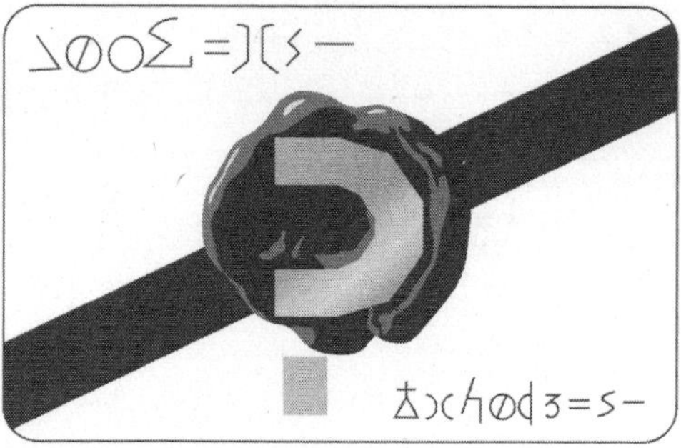

25a – *Remembrance of the Daleks*

'Lovely flowers begonias!'

Returning to Shoreditch, 1963, the Doctor and new chum Ace find Daleks waiting for them.

Not sure we can use Daleks.
It's for charity, but it *is* spoofing them. Risky.

Andy

* REMEMBER * Remove page before we go to print or we'll look like amateurs

Special Weapons Dalek (with weapons-grade plops)

80

Mike the Racist

There's a moment in the first episode where the adventure could have ended earlier for Ace. As the pair are walking back from Fertile Harry's café (more on his fertility later), Ace tries and fails to get to grips with pre-decimal money. Mike is at first mollified when Ace claims to come from Perivale, but when she struggles once more to comprehend pre-1970s currency, he asks whether she comes from 'somewhere else'. In Mike's language, as we later discover, that means 'are you a dirty foreigner?' Look at Mike's face as he asks – there's a cloud, momentarily, across his face. His eyes narrow and that friendly smile becomes a rictus. Faced with the possibility that the young bit of skirt he's just picked up might be one of them, Mike is torn between his usual Friday night pick-up act and sticking her on the first boat back to bongo bongo land, no doubt with a few bruises from when she 'fell down the stairs'.

Notice later that when Harry's at the hospital watching his wife give birth to their 17th child, the stand-in café manager is black. Mike, at this point, refuses to go near the place.

Four Bacon Sandwiches

It wouldn't be a Miwk **Doctor Who** book without this rant. Ace orders 'Four bacon sandwiches, one cup of coffee' and Harry repeats it back to her 'Four bacon sandwiches, one cup of coffee'.

How many sandwiches is that? Is that a single sandwich (made from two slices of bread) cut into four squares or triangles (Which do you prefer? Tell us on Twitter)? Or is it four sandwiches made from eight slices of bread? If it's the former, fair enough, but that's one bacon sandwich cut into four. If it's the latter then what the hell is that pig of a woman doing with all that pig meat and bread? She can't possibly finish four bacon sandwiches herself. It's possible one was for the Doctor but there's no sign of it when she and Mike head back to the school a little later. She must've eaten all four while Mike was trying to get into her knickers. Only one cup of coffee to wash down all that? Well, one cup of coffee and whatever Mike gave her. Nudge wink.

Just How Big Are Ace's Balls?

Having locked the Doctor in the basement of the school, leaving him to the (lack of) mercy of the Dalek therein, the headmaster is interfered with by Ace. His reaction is to knee her in the fanny. For our American readers, that means front bottom. Or lady parts. Or dirty bellows. No, not dirty bellows. That's wrong. Dirty *belows*. Weird. Microsoft Word keeps wanting to correct that to dirty bellows. Gonna leave that in if for no other reason than to keep up the word count.

He's a schoolteacher, a headmaster of a school in 1963. Now fair enough he's under Dalek control, but isn't that a bit of an over-reaction? He has no frame of reference to say Ace is anything but a near-school-age girl. Even the Daleks only recognise her as a 'small human female' – more on that later – so why on Earth does he knee her in the fantasy factory?

It's *possible* that Ace has balls. It's also possible that the Daleks have scanned her and identified her weak points but this doesn't confirm the presence of balls, merely a weak and poorly defended lady garden. If all the male villains in **Doctor Who** disabled the female companion by giving them a swift kick to the Vervoid's mouth, well we'd be in a fine old pickle.

Imagine Nero trying to overcome Barbara in *The Romans*. Not so funny now is it? Or the Master and Jo Grant. No hypnotism, just Delgado sticking the boot in until she agrees to take a bomb back to UNIT HQ. What about the Voc that attacks Toos in *Robots of Death*. Instead of his hand coming off he removes his foot and slings it at her lady's dematerialisation circuit.

Ace of course gets revenge by head-butting him in the penis. This plan could easily have backfired if he turned out to be the sort of bloke who gets turned on by abusing women.

His Mum Says He's Special

Let's consider the Special Weapons Dalek for a moment. The Daleks are a race prone to purity and superiority. Why then, would they construct a Dalek specifically called 'The Special Weapons Dalek'?

If Daleks can have guns that good, why haven't they all got them? It would make life a lot easier. They could blow away all kinds of shit with a honking great cannon like that strapped to their faces.

Does this mean that the other Daleks are categorised as 'Shit Weapons Daleks'? Because that's what they've made themselves. They have to cower behind this skanky, filthy old rust-bucket as it ka-blams seven shades of Kaled shit out of anything that gets in their way (for example, two lone Daleks or a pair of wooden doors which would never have withstood a volley of regular Dalek firepower).

The Time War would've been over a lot quicker with a few more of these bad bastards on-side. But where are they? They're nowhere to be seen. Instead the Daleks fight the war with Shit Weapons Daleks. The same old Shit Weapons Daleks they sent to guard an Icecano, the same old Shit Weapons Daleks they sent to bugger up Earth in 2150 or … whatever, the same old Shit Weapons Daleks they sent to a warehouse to... well we're not really sure. Do nothing other than create the problem they're trying to stop and um… stop a virus they've trapped on… with a time corridor that only operates between their own ship and… um… Save it for another book.

If we're going to have a 'Special Weapons Dalek' then henceforth all other Daleks should be rebranded as Shit Weapons Daleks and that branding should appear on toys, in print, on DVD (*Resurrection of the Shit Weapons Daleks, Destiny of the Shit Weapons Daleks, Power of the Shit Weapons Daleks, Shit Weapons Dalek etc.*) and even within in-story dialogue: 'I'm gonna wipe out every last stinking Shit Weapons Dalek out of the sky!'

What WOULD Happen if the Doctor Decided Nobody Should have Sugar?

In one of the more thoughtful pieces of dialogue in this story, the Doctor and Joseph the, café worker, muse on the issue of sugar and the nature of identity. Joseph says that his life may have been very different had the sugar and slave trade never happened. And he is right, he would have 'been an African', and may never have found himself serving up cups of tea to itinerant Time Lords on a dark November night in 1963.

But what would people have done for sugar? We would all acknowledge that slavery was (and indeed, in some parts of the world, still is) an evil practice, but it was part of the reason that the sugar trade took off and allowed sugar to become so dominant in Western society. Just think about all of the different things that we bung sugar into these days: sweets, chocolates, fizzy pop, ready meals, salami, breakfast cereals, tomato sauce, jam, bread, cakes, Pot Noodles, bakes beans, mints, medicines, yoghurt, salad dressings, soup, lollies, tea, coffee, ice cream, toffee, chewing gum, pickles, sugar cubes, cheese, doughnuts, sausages, pies, jelly and Kandy Men.

The answer to a lack of sugar is quite obvious really, and we must look again to the history of **Doctor Who** for the solution. If sugar hadn't have taken off, then people would have had to turn to other items to sweeten their food – such as honey. Goronwy and his fellow beekeepers would have been the saviours of the sweet tooth, and his little business would undoubtedly have prospered. The only problem with this would be that we would need *a lot* more bees than we are used to which would necessitate much more bee housing. This would have a knock-on effect of more land being required to house the hives, reducing the available space for housing, agriculture and other purposes. The increase would also probably have the unintended side effect of many more people being stung, with a negative resultant effect for the nascent National Health Service. But the whole slave thing wouldn't have happened, so that's good. The increase in the requirement for honey would also mean that the bees would have to seek out increasingly varied types of nectar from which they could create the honey. As there are only a certain amount of flowers on the planet then they would have to turn to other sources of nectar from plants that may result in rather odd or even unpleasant tasting varieties. A honey made predominantly from raspberry or blueberry would be rather nice we imagine, but one made from crab apple, thistles or chives probably wouldn't be.

Of course, honey used for human consumption is made by the

honeybee and it would have to be hoped that they could manage to keep up with human demand. If not, then types of honey made by other types of bees would possibly have to be considered as an alternative. We don't know if people would go for bumblebee honey or even it enough could be harvested. Certainly any processing plant would be a real hive of activity, buzzing with life.

Hang on a minute, if people had all of these poor insects working for us without any pay then isn't that merely another form of slavery? We're back where we started... Okay, if the Doctor had decided that nobody should have sugar, then we would just have to do without it.

Yes, But in Real World Terms, What *Would* Happen?

Well the next story would be buggered wouldn't it? Helen A is producing sugar in something like 3000 factories/refineries. If the Doctor had made that decision then there'd be no Kingston sales and no Happiness Patrol.

The Arrogance of the Doctor.

There's a swagger in the Doctor's step, and it's all because this time he's fully in control of events with a meticulously planned trap for the Daleks. That same plan would later come into force against the Cybermen – it's a good job both races aren't on speaking terms because the only difference between the two stories is the device the Doctor uses to dupe the half-witted aliens. But hey, it's a winning formula, so may as well go with it until the baddies catch on. The Doctor had also planned a similar fate for the Sontarans in an adventure which would have followed the second year. They would have been lured to the Earth of the 23rd Century where, at a private auction, The Braces of Sontar were being sold off to the highest bidder. Sontar, the last true Sontaran, before all that silly cloning business, is the hero of his race and it was for him that their home planet, originally called Papa Rellena, was renamed.

Needless to say, The Braces of Sontar aren't actual braces, no more than the Hand of Omega is a severed body part and the Silver Nemesis is white. They are, in fact, a superweapon of devastating power. The Braces are capable of wiping out whole planets in the blink of an eye (you can see where this is going, can't you?). The Sontarans were to have stormed the auction, devastating much of Southern England in the process, seized and primed the Braces to destroy Earth, home of the race which for no apparent reason the Sontarans have taken such a dislike to over the years. But, of course, it was all part of the Doctor's intricate (and same) plan. Substituting the co-ordinates of Earth for those of Sontar, the Braces would have destroyed the last remaining Sontarans and their home world in one fell swoop. The Doctor had even prepared a monologue about genetic diversity and homogenised milk.

But in *Remembrance of the Daleks* we see the Doctor's arrogance at his plan go unchecked. So self-satisfied is he that he constantly forgets to take care of minor details throughout the adventure. He allows Ace to leave the TARDIS with her ghetto blaster, only to chastise her later when the locals start to look at them funny. More seriously, we later see the Doctor and Ace take possession of a rocket launcher so that they can disable the Dalek transmat in the school cellar. Once Ace despatches the lone Dalek with their only shell he quickly forgets the whole idea. And so, a lone soldier dies on duty. The message has got through to Gilmore and his men that rocket launchers are effective against Daleks, albeit only the white and gold ones; the same weapon made nary a dent in the black and grey variety at Totters Lane, but as we shall later see, those Daleks are only vulnerable to house bricks.

The Pythtaker and the Undertakers

How exactly does the First Doctor drop the Hand of Omega off at the funeral parlour? Does he walk in one day with the casket and say, 'Can you hang on to this for me, please?' Surely undertakers are generally involved in the business of making and *filling* a casket, rather than just storing them? Can you imagine popping into the Co-op Funeral Care one day, having a chat with a black-suited minion and saying, 'I've brought a casket for you. It's already full.' Imagine their reaction. 'It's outside in the car. Yeah, yeah, she's already dead. Don't bother opening it though. I'm not a murderer, honest. Just keep it for me. *Whatever you do, don't look inside.*'

If it were us having that conversation and we were some sort of doctor, if it were us and definitely *not* the First Doctor having it as that would be horrendously in breach of copyright, if it were definitely *us*, Auton, having that conversation, we'd probably say something a bit like this:

Auton:	Good day, my boy!
Cockney Undertaker:	'Ello guv, what can I do for ya?
Auton:	Oh, I rather think you're the perfect man to help me. Hmm!
Cockney Undertaker:	Yes?
Auton:	Well, you see... someone's just, er... died, you see, and I've put them in that coffin there! Yes!
Cockney Undertaker:	You've put them in a coffin... yourself?

Auton:	It's nothing unusual, you know!
Cockney Undertaker:	It is a bit...
Auton:	She's definitely dead! I made sure of it.
Cockney Undertaker:	H-How did you?

(LONG PAUSE)

Cockney Undertaker:	Are you a... professional?

(LONG PAUSE)

Cockney Undertaker:	...like, are you perhaps a doctor or something?
Auton:	Oh, yes, I'm a doctor, yes! A doctor! Ho-ho! Now here's a gent I'm sure can help with my perfectly innocent casket.
Welsh Undertaker:	Yes, boyo?
Auton:	I have a casket here which I would like you young men to look after for me! My, my, quite extraordinary.
Cockney Undertaker:	Are you sure this is all above board, guv'nor?
Auton:	Yes, yes, yes, yes, yes. It's just my, er... grandmother! She died, you see, and...
Welsh Undertaker:	Your *grand*mother?
Auton:	Oh, stop all this shilly-shallying, Mr Over.. er, Undertaker, and bury it, will you!
Cockney Undertaker:	Thing is, mate, people usually ring us and we go round in our van and *collect* the bodies.

Auton:	She's definitely dead!
Cockney Undertaker:	I bet she is. We really can't take it, chief.
Auton:	I'm only trying to arrange for my casket to be left here, not start a jumble sale! This is an undertakers', isn't it?
Welsh Undertaker:	Yes, but–
Auton:	The lid's nailed down.
Cockney Undertaker:	I... I think we should open it, mate.
Auton:	Oh, I shouldn't think there's any need for that!
Cockney Undertaker:	We've really got to open it, mate.
Auton:	What's that, my boy? No, no, there's no need to open it, you see. I'm not a murderer! And anyway, I hate killing!
Welsh Undertaker:	It's just that there's a problem, boyo.
Auton:	And what's that, eh?
Welsh Undertaker:	Well, there are rules about this sort of thing, there are!
Auton:	You know, I really believe I have underestimated you two young men. Now, you wouldn't object to holding a casket for a dear old gentleman like me, would you? Hm?
Cockney Undertaker:	Nah, mate... it's just...
Auton:	Oh, I'm not buggering about here all day, and anyway, I have places to be!
Welsh Undertaker:	That could be for the best, it is.
Auton:	Then I shall go. But one day, I shall come back... one day. Until then, there must be...

Cockney Undertaker:	Can you leave now please?
Auton:	Yes.
Welsh Undertaker:	There's lovely.

On the other hand, perhaps the undertakers take whatever work they can get in such difficult times. In many ways it's a dying industry.

The Daleks and Little Girls

As we saw in *Destiny of the Shit-Daleks*, the Daleks have somehow come under the impression that they are now robotic life-forms, driven by logic. And with two Dalek factions fighting for supremacy, they find themselves in much the same situation as they did with the Movellans back on Skaro – locked in stalemate, each side anticipating the other's next scissor, paper or stone.

And so, once again, the 'black' Daleks require a random factor to help them break their logical thinking and generate some creative thinking. We'll come to just how the Daleks managed to forget that they are anything but logical in a moment, but for now let's just go along with their fatally misguided scheme.

In secreting the Hand of Omega on Earth, the Doctor has given the Daleks little choice in terms of selecting their wildcard. Of all the life-forms on the planet, humans have the most developed brains and so a human it must be. But what kind of human? A strategist like Gilmore wouldn't do – he's far too constrained by his military training. Ratcliffe and his followers are too blinkered. No, the Daleks needed to get *really* creative and that means only one thing: a pre-pubescent girl.

Fickle, flighty, boundlessly imaginative, young girls are a fount of creative thinking – no idea is too big, too ambitious, too silly – they see the world through unblinkered eyes and they are too young to have the slightest ounce of cynicism. A little girl is the perfect solution to the Daleks' problems. In the 6 months since they tethered the poor child to their Davros-in-a-Crash-Helmet device, she has devised no less than 11 different schemes to break the deadlock between the Daleks:

> Space unicorns which fire death rays from their horns
>
> Flowers that smell like poo
>
> Hide the other Daleks' toys
>
> Tell Davros' mum on him
>
> Tell the headmaster that she saw Audrey Simpkins from 5B buying cigarettes from one of them
>
> Big dolls that cry *really* loud and hurt their ears
>
> Get bad men to steal the Doctor's gun and use that
>
> A Glitter Gun (ultimately this idea fell into other hands)
>
> Build more robots but make them better
>
> Sweets that make them sick
>
> Play hide and seek with them but they hide first and you trick them by not looking

With a little tweaking, the Daleks chose option 7 and the rest is history.

But what of the fatal flaw in the Daleks' logic? That they

themselves are logic-based creatures with no capacity for creative thinking outside of the capabilities of their enemies? Well that, as we all know, is a load of old (Donald) tosh. The Daleks are *not* robots and there's never been the slightest sign that they even know what logic is, let alone that they're driven by it. The Daleks we know are hate-filled little cans who trundle about the place shrieking like hysterical children whenever they don't get their own way.

If Daleks were logical, when they said 'exterminate' they would do just that and you'd be dead. Instead, the Daleks have to fill-in for a few minutes while poor old Ace fumbles with her rocket launcher, pissing herself with fear while three of them round on her, screeching the word over and over. The Daleks like to toy with their prey – they're quick to fire when taken by surprise or where there's a chance their prey might escape, such as when Ace escapes from the lab and runs down the stairs, but when they're really sure they can't miss the Daleks like to have a bit of fun and make sure that their victim is absolutely scared out of their wits before dealing the final blow. It's the closest a Dalek can get to a sexual thrill, caged up, as they are, in their impenetrable casings and, deviants that they are, they really get off on it. The Daleks are anything but logical. They're capricious, hate-fuelled bastards who love nothing more than tormenting their victims before destroying them.

So, again, you can see why they went for the kid. Kindred spirits.

Ace's Stench

Does Ace stink or does she smell super-fresh? She seems to get through a hell of a lot of deodorant.

Ratcliffe's Little White Lies

Ratcliffe proudly stands up as a racist. His claims that Britain supported the wrong side in the Second World War are testament to that, as are The Association's other activities. We don't see them actually come out and say the word because that would demand courage and as we all know 'ists' generally don't have the eloquence or the courage to really speak up for themselves in a calm, measured way and give the rest of us a chance to point and laugh at them.

But Ratcliffe has allied himself with the ultimate dirty foreigners in siding with the Daleks. Blinded, possibly, by their promises of power, he throws out all his ideals and mucks in with a race who come not from over the Channel or from bongo bongo land, but from outer bloody space. It doesn't get more foreign than that. Perhaps it is the call of familiarity which ties Ratcliffe to the renegade Daleks? At their core, the Daleks are driven by rampant xenophobia and seek to eradicate all lesser species (by which, as we've seen so many times before, they mean 'all' species). Clearly they aren't going to let Ratcliffe in on that part of their plan because when it comes to fascism, the Daleks are properly committed. Ratcliffe, on the other hand is simply an embittered old idiot who fights for no cause other than the supremacy of himself and his mates. Racist, fascist, ageist, sexist…whatever it takes to get ahead, if he can tie his flag to that cause then that's okay with him. Things were bad enough for Ratcliffe before the war, but during the post-war reconstruction when the Empire flung open her doors to allow immigrants to come and help get Britain back on its feet, the poor sap lost all sense of reality and simply allied himself with a superior force which seemed to offer a shortcut to his strongest desire – England for the English. He wouldn't have thought any further than that tasty carrot.

Doctor: War Bastard

In blowing up Skaro, did the Doctor just start the Time War? Pretty much, yep. All that emotional wrangling the 8th Doctor did before throwing himself into the war, the 9th Doctor's existential angst at destroying his own people, the 10th Doctor's devastation at being the only one of his kind, the 11th Doctor's uncontrollable hands…all these things are the result of his own fannying about in the first place.

Density of the Daleks

One of the curious things about *Remembrance of the Daleks* is that the villains of the piece – or at least one of them – have started to specify the size, species and sex of their victims. In the scene in the school the Dalek who discovers Ace says: 'small human female sighted on Level 3'. This instruction is presumably being relayed to the Dalek mother ship, but the instructions are hardly that precise. Different countries for example, have different numbering systems for the levels of a building. In the UK, the ground floor is the one at which you enter a building. In the USA, however, this floor is known as the First Floor. The Daleks may use an entirely different arrangement. If the Dalek to whom this information is being relayed had any sense then it would query it.

Also, the Dalek would need to know just how small 'small' is in this case. As they encounter numerous species on numerous planets, the Daleks really should have some Dalek-standard units of measurement. 'Small' tells them nothing. Small in relation to what precisely? Does the Dalek in the school mean 'shrunk by the Master' small or 'Mr Sin' small? Dalek Command would need to have this information in order to know whether they would need to deploy more normal Daleks or if they need to call upon the services of the Special Weapons Dalek. Perhaps the Dalek that finds Ace is just being ultra-pernickety and has taken it upon itself to go into too much detail in an effort to impress Davros? This one could be the Dalek equivalent of the precocious, crawling child who takes his teacher an apple into school.

Of course, if Daleks had to come up with a standard of measurement relative to size they could call them rels. Or different sorts of rel: size-rel, time-rel, space-rel, weapon-shitness-rel...

This aside, you have to wonder if there has been a new Dalek directive introduced that requires them to describe everything they encounter in all instances. A policy such as this would generate a huge amount of paperwork for the Daleks back in the office. Do they have to do it *every* time they see a target? What happens if they just happen to see a spider? Would they have to say: 'averaged-sized arachnid of indeterminate gender sighted crawling up a wall?' They couldn't possibly obtain all of the details of the spider because it would probably be too small to tell what sex it was. Is it only living things that they have to do this for, or does everything that they encounter that they may perceive to be a threat have to be described? 'Large green chair sighted on the Ground Floor', 'Several large sausages seen on plate in canteen'. What if they trundled past a television set showing series three of **Alias**? 'Bristow is a spy, her dad is good, no he's bad, no he's good, no he's bad, uh-oh, Sark's back and so is thingy from series four. Small plot discrepancy observed in twelfth minute, crash zoom out of place in scene fourteen…'

All of this could of course merely be a foible of this one particular Dalek, but if it is then his line manager needs to have a word with him because he is acting out of step.

What Year Ith Thith?

In fact, forget the year! What month is this? What time of day is it? Mike's mum's telly (which is black and white, but we knew that from the helpful signage in her window) wheezes into life and announces a new science fiction serial called 'Do-'. We're meant to believe this is **Doctor Who** which is fair enough.

Ace has washed her hair and everyone's gone out for the day. It's bright outside and given the First Doctor's recent departure, we're presuming it's November or thereabouts. There's a calendar visible in one shot that says it's November. So it's November, and the telly says it's 5.15 and while it doesn't say whether that's AM or PM, since the BBC didn't broadcast until 11am at the earliest, it must be 5.15pm or 1715hrs as Gilmore might say to sound chunky-sexy.

The clear and simple answer is that the Daleks have moved the sun. This is probably why they need the Hand of Omega, itself a 'stellar manipulator'. It's nothing evil or nasty, they just want to pop the sun back where it was. They're essentially a very tidy species. You never see much in the way of Dalek mess.

Speaking of Dalek mess – do Daleks poo? They're organic internally so there must be some sort of ingestion process that occurs. Not only must they poo, they must eat too. So Dalek dinners must be served somewhere, presumably in the Dalek canteen. They feed the Robomen little food pills in the international box office smash **Shit Daleks' Invasion Earth 2150AD**. Maybe their suckers can be used to suck up those little pills?

So where does the poo go? Well they're sealed inside their casings and they're also bloody angry. It's possible Davros buggered up this side of their design and the casings just fill up over time. That would certainly make us pretty angry. Loud noises can often cause sensitive people to crap their pants. Would this explain why the Special Weapons Dalek is covered in all that crap? Every time he fires that bloody great cannon he craps himself and it's spilling out the top.

It may also explain their change of colour scheme over the years. Once utterly soiled in Krusted Kaled Krap they need a drain and a re-spray.

Tick another mystery box off as solved. Good god – this book was worth every penny, wasn't it?

25b – *The Happiness Patrol*

'Big schmiles, girlsch! It'sch schowtime!'

On a distant Earth colony, a leader tries desperately to get everyone to cheer up a bit. Or die.

> THE FIRST INTERNATIONAL CONFERENCE
> FOR PEOPLE CALLED
> # **SUSIE**

Work it out yourself.

The Nomenclature of Terra Alpha

The naming conventions of the colony are subject to some scrutiny. Each colonist displays a twentieth century forename and an individual letter as a surname. This letter appears to indicate rank, with Helen A at the top, rather than her just being called 'Helen Atkinson' or something. This further implies a pyramidal structure to the society, with a single 'A' figure and presumably many 'Z' figures (if they survived).

Why then is Helen's domestic partner, Joseph, only a C grade? Again, unless his surname is really Chesterton, he is not considered to be of similar rank as Helen A. This may be a result of his apparent status as a civilian. So who holds a B grade? Perhaps there really are just no Mr Barringtons or Mr Benson-Phillipses on Terra Alpha? But if we take the rank idea as read, the lack of a Gordon B or Polly B is telling. Presumably Helen A had them done away with or she just never promotes anybody to a rank close to her own. The lack of such checks and balances in Helen A's unusual regime is a worrying indicator of her position.

How did this all begin then? Let us posit a scenario: a new colony is created by Helen A's (recent) ancestors. With little indication of who should administer this colony, two competing systems develop: democratic elections are favoured by many of the colonists but are ultimately considered inadequate given the detailed workings of the society. An alternative plan is put into place: that of pulling letters out of a Scrabble bag to decide importance. Scrabble is clearly a key part of Terra Alphan society, probably starting out as something interesting to do on the rocket over from Vasilip or wherever. Even now, every summer there are grand Scrabble games in the Place de la Logos, with a huge Scrabble board painted on the (shiny flat) ground and human players forming the letters.

During one memorable game in the summer of '84, Suzie Q, Jenny U, Ian I, Bertie X, Norman T, Alan I and Audrey C stood next to Vincent O to form the word Quixotic on a triple letter score. That was worth 324 points plus 50 for using up all the people on the rack. Unfortunately Bertie X was also one of the players in the game and was unable to continue to participate after using himself on the board. Bertie X subsequently lost the game to Jeff F 375 points to 821.

The game continues to prosper in the colonies. However, 'Terra Alphan rules' Surname Scrabble is considered to be exceedingly difficult, as unlike regular Scrabble, there's only one A.

Other famous residents of Terra Alpha include Jack D, Peter K, Gina G, Deep Blue C, Mel B, Mr T, Anita P, Honey B, Bobby V, Jor-L and Jay-Z. Oh, and Hots X.

Sweets for My Sweet

When considering The Kandy Man we must look at how he is constructed. Gilbert M built him out of a particular brand of confectionary – let's call them 'Liquorice Allsorts' – which are vastly oversized in comparison to the ones that you, being a tubby sweet-munching sort, and I (use them mainly for bribery, never for personal use) can buy in the shops.

So, how exactly were these larger versions created? Did Gilbert make the component parts from existing 'off the shelf' Allsorts from shops on Terra Alpha, or were they made specifically for the purpose of creating the Kandy Man? If the former is what happened, then it makes us wonder just why the population needed such large confectionary and also how they managed to eat them? The Allsorts would need to be carved up into much smaller pieces for consumption and you have to question if an average family would even manage to get through them all. Unless the Pipe People, in their non-starved form have really, really big mouths. Wider than a large tunnel or a lake. Do you just buy one sweet at a time, or do you get a massive bag with the usual mixed assortment?

The torso of the Kandy Man is made from what looks like a huge boiled sweetie, but no normal human could ever get something so huge into his or her mouth. Also, wouldn't huge sweets attract huge ants? Does the Kandy Man live in fear of Zarbi? It would take *ages* to get through an entire bag of massive Allsorts and a massive boiled sweet would end up with hair and fluff stuck all over it. This must be why the Kandy Man doesn't wear a coat or sweater.

How would these packets of massive sweeties be displayed in the shops? Stores would have to be enormous to accommodate this oversized confectionary. And how would you get such large packets of sweets home from the shops? Are you given a massive carrier bag to put them in? Maybe that's what those go-karts are for? Other, everyday things would have to be greatly increased in size to deal with big sweets. The family car would need to be more like a wagon just in order to accommodate one product. A huge bag of Allsorts in the back of your wagon alongside your normal size tin of beans, loaf of bread, fruit and veg, cotton buds, Anusol etc. would just be weird. When you got this gargantuan bag of sweets home where would a Terra Alphan keep them? We keep our sweets on the kitchen bench sometimes, but what size kitchen bench would you need to put Kandy Man-size sweets on? You couldn't prepare any meals in your kitchen because it would be covered in colossal sweets. And ants.

Why did Gilbert build the Kandy Man anyway? Did he need a

chief executioner and didn't want to get his own hands sticky? Or was the Kandy Man, as we suspect, a grim sex toy gone awry?

If the sweets were made especially by Gilbert M purely for the purpose of constructing his lover, then he would have had to go to the expense, trouble and cost of building a special production line just for this one particular manufacturing task. He's got quite a plummy voice so we reckon he had the money to do this. But would it not have been easier to try to meet somebody in the normal way, rather than embarking on this crackpot scheme? Gilbert M's is quite a grand idea considering that the machinery used in the Kandy Man's construction would probably only ever be used once. Where was the massive sweet-making factory located? Somewhere on Terra Alpha is there a flippin' great Willy Wonka palace with tiny Oompa Loompas engaged in vital sugary sex doll research? A construction project on this scale would be huge, just imagine the costs associated with it: there'd be material to buy and workers to pay, not to mention all of the galactic-colony council bureaucracy to get past. You simply can't build a factory of that size, because *it makes no sense*. There is very little hands-on consideration in any of Gilbert's plan and it seems that he was hell bent on creating this monstrous deviant without any practical thought for the infrastructure, government budget or consequences for the workforce who would be needed to carry out this ludicrous scheme.

What's more, one use and it'd be stuck to the sheets forever.

Pick 'n' Mix m'Bits

The Kandy Man is composed mainly of Liquorice Allsorts, a boiled sweet and some sticks of rock. We feel Gilbert was short-sighted in his choice of sweets. The Kandy Gigolo could have been made much more impressive, and dare we say *realistic* had a wider range of sweets been used in his manufacture. Here are some things that could have been used to improve his creation:

> Liquorice shoelaces – these could be used as hair (head, armpit and scrotal), or for shoelaces. A crude beard could even be fashioned for the Kandy Man, which would be far better than the metal whisker plate thing that he sports here. What sort of sweet is that made from Gilbert? You failure.
> Chewing gum pellets – for use as teeth. Carefully arranged, the 'goofy vicar' effect could be achieved in order to make him appear less threatening. Or you could just use those false teeth. He might look a bit like an Osmond though.
> Jazzies – to add a touch of authenticity, these could be stuck on various parts of the body to simulate a skin rash or STD.
> Gobstobbers – eyes. Gobstoppers of increasing size can be used to measure increased levels of incredulity or anger. He whips one set out and quickly shoves another set in.
> Lion Bars – could be used if we ever need to see the Kandy Man at the toilet.
> Aero bars – could be used if we ever need to see the Kandy Man at the toilet, furiously trying to get rid of something that won't flush away.
> Various coloured soft drinks – could be used to represent different types of wee wee. A normal one could be depicted with lemon juice, a nasty infection could be shown with cloudy traditional-style lemonade and cranberry juice could be used for a more serious condition, again implying an STD.
> Green midget gems – slightly melted, these could

represent boils.
Flying Saucers – nipples (fizzy).
Foam mushrooms – also a possibility for nipples (non-fizzy).
Pink shrimp – winky. For use when he is cold or on the flop.
Sherbet Fountain – also could be used for the cock. It would be interchangeable with the pink shrimp, depending on what the Kandy Man is getting up to that day. The Sherbet Fountain also has the advantage of being able to be 'extended' by tugging on the liquorice stick and can 'shoot' out its contents if squeezed or jerked. It should fit the Kandy Man since it, too, is made by Bassett's.
2 x Ferrero Rocher – balls. Can be moistened and rolled in sweet tobacco if hairier variety is required.
1 x Toffifee – arsehole. This is the bit where poo comes out (cf. Aero, Lion Bar)
Sugar paper – pallid skin.
Funny Feet ice cream lollies – feet. These would have to remain frozen, so a miniature freezer unit would have to be installed into the legs. Or Terra Alpha could be moved to Iceworld.

We think that everybody would agree that if any of the above items were used to build a Kandy Man then the resulting being would look far better, sweeter and sexier than the one Gilbert M came up with.

Terror Alpha

Being happy is, as we all know, compulsory on Terra Alpha. The consequences of not wearing a permanent smile are, not to mince words, final. Helen A and her government don't make it easy for the denizens of that most joyous of worlds. The tactic of forcing everyone to feign happiness should really be a last resort. There are much more effective ways of jollying along the population, even if you're still determined to bleed them dry:

1. Make 'em laugh. Muzak isn't everyone's cup of tea, but a bit of jolly music piped over the airwaves would work wonders. But put some effort into it – get a personable DJ (Or Dee J) to host the tunes, play a variety of upbeat tracks (we recommend anything by Bernard Cribbins) or even mix things up with a few radio comedies, a la Radio 4 Extra. Wes Butters and his gang do a great job of lifting the nation's spirits with repeats of **Hancock's Half Hour**, **Round the Horne** and other choice morsels from the BBC archive. Why not do the same? It's hard enough to maintain a happy face when all you want to do is have a good cry, but try being miserable when you've got the finest comedians in the world giving it their all. Radio Alpha, let's call it, wouldn't necessarily be an expensive venture – after all, there are no costly production values required; just a few talented writers (we'd have done it for the exposure alone, but this book is indicative of our lack of talent in this area), some decent performers and a microphone.

2. Spruce the place up a bit. Grey walls, grey floors, black street furniture. Seasonal affective disorder (SAD) does exactly what the name implies – when your environment is drab and grim your mood is too. Those half-arsed attempts to paint things pink simply aren't enough. Why not paint the floors yellow and the walls a nice crisp white? Maybe with a few flowers here and there for decoration? Even something as simple as painting the benches red did wonders for passengers on Britain's railways. Sitting around waiting for a train for four hours is made just a little more pleasant when you're sitting on a jolly red bench (or

Kang). These are all small changes, but the cumulative effect would be enormous.

3. In fact a bit of greenery wouldn't go amiss either. The money you could save on dolly birds with big guns would be much better spent on a few trees and pot plants about the place.

4. See 2. Light! Maybe the days are full of sunshine, but there's no evidence of that here as the story takes place at night, so how about installing a few more street lights?

5. In much the same vein, allowing shops to sell dark clothing is something of a no-no, too. The first character we see has a lovely sunny top on but it's hidden by that dark overcoat. Polka dot rain macs or nice beige tweed would do wonders. It's hard to be happy when you're dressed like you're on your way to a funeral.

6. If you will insist on having dolly birds with big guns as your enforcers, make them less threatening. Helen A's attitude is more carrot than stick, and that's simply never going to work in the long term. Fear breeds resentment. Send the patrols to a workshop-or-two and have them learn about basic motivational techniques like being nice, saying 'hello' to passers-by, the power of a cheery wave every now and then. Anything which says 'we're going to hurt you if you don't cheer up, but we'll do whatever we can to help you first'. This could back-fire on the more perverted citizens.

7. Implement a fixed period every week when it's okay to be miserable – a catharsis for the population, enabling them to get all their frustration, anger and misery out in one big push. You could call it Sadness Sunday (Or 'PanoptiCon'). In fact, why not go the whole hog and name the other days of the week in amusing ways? Water-balloon Wednesdays would be great fun, Slapstick Saturdays, Funny Fridays – that sort of thing. But not Mime Mondays, that would have the wrong effect entirely.

You'd pretty soon end up with Murderous Monday and nobody wants that.

8. Silas P is a nasty old bugger, but his opening gambit of 'do you want to talk about it?' is precisely what the likes of him should be doing. A counselling service would go down a storm with a population so downtrodden. Just venting can make a huge difference and combined with a little cognitive behaviour therapy, the unfortunate sufferers could find better ways to cope with their problems. Simply telling people that there's a place they can go to for help and then duping them into confessing they're feeling a bit down is just plain nasty.

9. Ditch the clown make-up. Nobody really likes clowns, do they? (We bet Ace does though) And yet all government officials and civil servants are caked in foundation and rouge and have silly coloured hair. If it's designed to put people on edge, then it works, but if the desired effect is anything other than that, then it's sorely misjudged.

The Happiness Patrol

The fatal flaw in the Happiness Patrol's raison d'être, as pointed out by the Doctor is that they can't shoot you if you appear to be happy, no matter how forced that happiness is. So why don't the population just stick on a smile whenever they find themselves at the wrong end of a gun?

The same 'twisted logic' as pointed out by the Doctor means that a pissed off Happiness Patroller is herself subject to execution or imprisonment. It's fair to say that there's a lack of logic at work generally on Terra Alpha, but the rules of engagement for The Happiness Patrol are madness, pure and simple.

Has nobody honestly ever given any thought to this before? Apparently over half a million people haven't. Half a million really quite stupid people, as it turns out. We were expecting the Doctor to have a grand scheme to bring down the government but in reality all he has to do is deflect the Patrol by putting on a happy face and give Helen A a bit of a talking to. Killing her favourite pet helped, but as murder is against the Doctor's moral code, we'll have to assume that's just a fortunate coincidence and that his helping Earl Sigma attract Fifi and shatter the candy with the right resonant notes was done out of nothing more than his desire, much as he had back on Gallifrey as a child, to enjoy some subterranean homesick blues.

We're sorry you had to read all that for one bad joke.

Punishments

During this story we witness a Terra Alphan dissident (called Cy T) suffering a terrible fate when he is executed by being drowned in a vast quantity of fondant. Now, while the The Fondant Surprise must be an awful way to go it is pure folly on the part of the Kandy Man to carry out such a theatrical, wasteful punishment. As a confectioner and businessman the top and bottom of things for him must surely be his profit margin? Wantonly squandering resources in this manner would be bound to cut into his earnings. This killing is nothing other than *Grand Guignol* for the sake of appearances. If the Kandy Man and Gilbert M had really thought things through, then they could have come up with some equally dreadful punishments that wouldn't have adversely affected the company's books. Let's consider some of the things that should have been on the drawing board:

The Hot Fudge Injection – as we know from cutting ourselves humans have blood in their veins, and what better way to get rid of somebody than by replacing the blood with molten fudge? It would be quite an easy task to set up a syringe filled with boiling hot fudge or some kind of intravenous infusion to get the stuff into the body. Cheaper than the sodium thiopental.

The Candy Floss Teddy Bear – the guilty party is filled up through the mouth with lots and lots of candyfloss until he suffocates and is turned into a grotesque parody of a teddy bear. Candyfloss is just sugar and with the economies of scale associated with sugar purchasing in a confectionary plant, they could do this one really cheaply.

Death by Candy Cane – this is a nasty one. The victim is harnessed face down on a hard bed, and candy canes are inserted into all his or her holes. This isn't the worst of it though as the diameter of the canes is increased at regular intervals until the victim is 'widened' at all points until they are burst.

Caramel Shards – caramel can be dangerous stuff both in its hot and cold states. When molten it can cause quite severe burns if it accidentally gets onto the skin, and when cooled it can shatter and form sharp shards that can lacerate. We've visited a sweet factory and seen the amount of wastage that production can generate. As all of the off-cuts and trimmings can't be sold directly to the public, then why not make better use of them for the purpose of retribution? Perhaps some form of 'bed of shards' could be devised?

Toffee Brittle – the prisoner's head is coated in hot toffee and nuts which is then left to set before a group of hungry and rabid squirrels are let loose on them.

Chocolate Helmet of Terror – similar to the above, but here a pan of seething hot chocolate is placed over the head of the victim, and allowed to set over the face thus preventing him from being able to breathe. It's a bit like when you used to get that chocolate sauce to squirt onto an ice cream, which would then set hard on it - only with added death.

Sugar Roulette – a death sentence devised purely for use on diabetic victims. The prisoner would be presented with a series of jars, five of which would contain sugar and one that contains salt. They would have to pick a jar from which they would have to eat all of the contents on a big spoon. If they get salt then they get to live, otherwise they are left to their fate. Although eating a jar of salt probably won't do you any favours either.

Sherberting – the victim is fitted with two large straws that are inserted into the nostrils. The mouth is sealed up with sticky tape and the straws are connected to a hopper full of extra-fizzy sherbet, which is pumped into the victim at two-minute intervals. After two minutes of sherbeting, the pump is switch off and the victim has two minutes of no sherbet before the device is activated again. This is repeated until the victim's head has exploded.

The Custard Blowback – too disgusting to go into.

This is merely a selection of punishments that we have come up with, but anybody with a bit of a twisted mind could probably come up with some more appalling examples. Put your mind to it and see what devilish sentences you can think of!

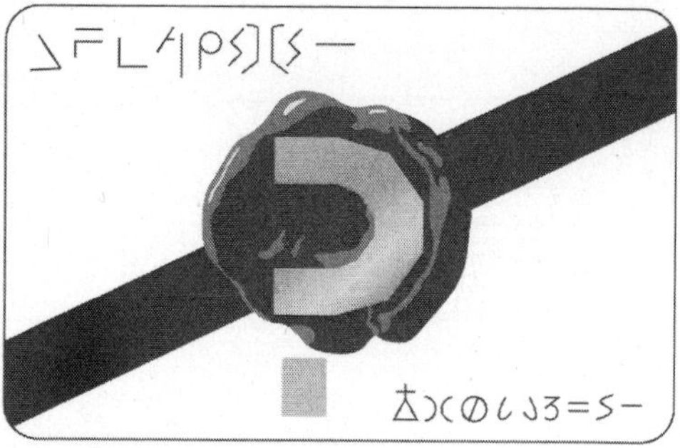

25c – *Silver Nemesis*

> *'We ride to destiny!'*

A Nazi with a bow and a loony with an arrow get caught up in jazz, safari parks, Cybermen and social workers.

Cyberleader craps his pants when he hears 'Gold' on the wireless.

Together in Electric Screams

Digital watches were cool once. You'd wear them out in the open and people wouldn't throw stones at you or lunge at you with knives. You'd be the coolest cat in town, strutting your stuff down the High Street in your ace gear.

At critical points during the day, especially on each hour, your brilliant watch would beep twice telling you that it was one o'clock, two o'clock, three o'clock or whatever o'clock it was. You'd immediately look at your watch to see what time it was because it could be that you've been doing whatever you've been doing for far too long and the beep-beep might signify two o'clock when you thought it was eleven o'clock.

However it soon got boring and the beep-beep of a digital watch is something you can't turn off. It would happen at least once during any trip to the cinema or theatre. In school you could try and synchronise all the watches in one class so they'd go off simultaneously. Often this would require setting them five minutes early just in case they went off when you were already leaving the lesson. We drove many teachers insane with this.

But then comes the time at a funeral when a particularly moving eulogy is being read and all those watches start going off at staggered intervals like drunken, horny, digital crickets.

The watches had to go. They were annoying, they were pointless and we managed to replace them with something much less annoying in the mobile phone.

Anyway, the point is: If you were Karl, wouldn't you switch off that bloody annoying beeping noise his computer plays when displaying a date and time? Has Karl even got his grid references correct? On the computer screen that he looks at in

their South American hideaway, it states that Windsor is located at 74°W, 32°N. Not on any map we know it isn't. Those coordinates take you to somewhere in the Atlantic Ocean, just off the coast of Florida. The actual latitude and longitude coordinates for Windsor are 0° 36'W, 51°28'N because we went to the effort of looking it up.
And these people are trying to take over the world?

De Flores Tiles

De Flores is a Nazi right? He has been hiding out in South America somewhere since the end of the Second World War, like Martin Bormann and Ludwig Kessler did. We can assume that he was assisted in his flight from the crumbling Reich by ODESSA, so he must be using a pseudonym to disguise his true identity. 'Flores' is a Spanish word that means 'flowers', and not a German surname. Clearly he has either chosen this identity because 'flowers' sounds all nice and non-threatening and would be unlikely to draw attention to himself, or his father was a fascist Spaniard. We think that De Flores is a bit of a dandy in comparison to some of the other Nazis, so perhaps he thinks that the name reflects his personality in some way.

If he hadn't been as wise then he would possibly have used a name like 'El Malvado' or 'El Malicioso' or 'De la Raza Superior' or 'Villano malvado en el servicio de los Cybermen', so he did very well to disguise his intentions by using such a pleasant-sounding, friendly name. His real German name is 'Gunther von der Vornehm Halstuch'.

But look at the state of his house! Is this hotchpotch of old tat really suitable for a proposed leader of the Master Race? It seems all very fancy and a trifle odd, more like a museum than somewhere that you could live. His office is decorated with all of that Nazi paraphernalia and Wagner is blaring out from the gramophone. Do we suppose that he listens to Wagner all of the time, or merely when he is formulating plans for the Fourth Reich? Did De Flores bring all of this stuff with him when he fled Germany or has he bought it since he left? We bet that Hitler didn't even take his work home with him like this. The chess motif on the floor is an interesting touch. Given that the Seventh Doctor's era has something of an overarching chess theme we suppose that somebody might have been able to have a game on De Floor. Oh, and the decoration on his ceiling is awful. Despite his rather strange taste in decoration, it is clear that the man is a monster – he was going to shoot that nice parrot for goodness sake.

Sneeze-a-geddon

It's allergy season once the Seventh Doctor appears on the scene. In just six stories we have four sneezing fits. Clearly something the Rani slipped him in that drug cocktail has made him and all those around him susceptible to dust.

While he's hiding in the laundry room with Ray – the dirty sod – he sneezes his way into the Bounty Hunter's lap due to some dusty old shelves. ('Haha, did you know that in the novelisation…?' yes we did – shut up).

As we know, Time Lords are able to share some of their gifts with those they travel with which explains why Ace suddenly likes jazz and how Sarah Jane can understand Italian. An additional gift passed on to Melanie, known as Mel, is this terrible sneezing problem. In *Dragonfire* Melanie, known as Mel, nearly gives away her and Ace's excellent hiding place under a see-through floor grate. Great grate that. But Ace also succumbs in *Silver Nemesis* necessitating some quick-thinking on the Doctor's part where he immediately imitates birds that in no way sound like a sneeze. This may also be a previously unseen Time Lord ability.

The Doctor's tickly nose nearly gets the better of him in *Remembrance of the Daleks* as he and Ace hide behind some tent flaps. Did you giggle at 'flaps'? Pathetic.

This Doctor does of course carry a handkerchief around in his top pocket but at no point does he make use of it to blow his nose. It covers his mouth as he sniffs a Dalek's insides, it cleans his hand when he gets it covered in sticky fruity mess on Segonax and spit-wipes Ace's face clean in *The Curse of Fenric*.

Someone should show him what it's for. Maybe then he'd stop with all the sneezing.

The Naffness of De Flores

Hidden in a South American bolthole since fleeing Germany at the end of the Second World War, De Flores' excitement at the impending Fourth Reich is unbearable by the time he finally reaches Britain on his quest to secure the Nemesis statue. He's like a little Hitler Youth on Heiligabend, barely able to contain himself. But, he's waited over forty years, so a few more hours should be kinderspiel. Not so, however. Somehow the gang have cleared customs at Heathrow with a stash of machine pistols, army regalia, presumably a few swastikas for later, a suitcase full of cravats and a 'silver' bow which, let's face it, is probably due some import tax of some kind.

Anyone aware of the Nazis, the Second World War and the films of Leni Riefenstahl will know that the Nazis were bloody good at putting on a show. They rarely looked slapdash. So why on Earth has De Flores skanked on the budget by renting a crappy old blue Transit van? It doesn't exactly scream elegance does it? They can't even use the excuse that they don't want to attract attention since they're all dressed up in military uniforms and carrying guns. Surely some sort of caterpillar-tracked vehicle or army camouflage limousine would've been more suitable?

Because if there's one thing the Nazis really understood it was the importance of putting on a show. Wars have been won and lost on the strength of a proper uniform and there's no way De Flores was going to let victory slip through his grasp by letting any of his men wear anything less than the full kit. In fact his only concession was a giant swastika on the side of his van. However, a five foot swastika was indeed emblazoned across the side of the vehicle, but to deter potential onlookers, they kept it hidden under a sheet, carefully dyed the same shade of blue and glued to the side of the van with Uhu. The plan was to proudly sweep away the sheet on arrival in Windsor, but the Doctor's untimely arrival threw De Flores' gang off guard and they forgot to unveil their proud symbol. De Flores was, from that point on, doomed to certain failure.

Ace's Many Frustrations

'Oh' moans Ace, as usual, 'I hate when people's alarms go off at gigs'.

Run that one by us again, Dorothy? You *hate* when people's *alarms* go off at *gigs*?

We're **Doctor Who** fans. We don't go to that many gigs, but we've been to at least nine we can think of and that's just music gigs. Comedy gigs as well, possibly thirty or forty.

At no point during any of those gigs do we recall an alarm going off except at a Beautiful South one in Brixton where a fire alarm was set off and nobody left the building, the band played on. It didn't spoil the gig, it made it.

Oh sure, we've heard phones go off at gigs. We've heard people make a call during a film and a play, we even saw a guy with an Apple device 'face time' someone during **The Lego Movie**. But none of these people's alarms went off. And even if they did, the very nature of most gigs is that they're loud. Ace, who let's face it, doesn't seem like a jazz girl, would generally go to loud gigs. Listen to the crap she likes in *Remembrance of the Daleks*. Would you really hear someone's pocket watch alarm going off over that racket?

Maybe Ace means pagers? She is after all from 1985(ish), and it's always possible there were a lot of pagers going off around then, but even then who would actually respond to one? Except Grace if she was on call.

Yet again this is Ace having a moan about something that doesn't need to be moaned about. And don't get us started on why the weather's so fucking lovely on the 23rd November 1988 – look it up, it wasn't.

The 'Silver' Nemesis

Who or what is the eponymous silver nemesis? Nemesis is called Nemesis but is patently not silver, while the Cybermen are silver-ish and technically a Nemesis but only of the Doctor and with Nemesis the statue in the story surely she/it outranks the Cybermen as a nemesis in this instance?

It's more likely that the title refers to those two silver-haired old men in headphones who wander around open-air jazz concerts *wearing headphones* and holding silenced pistols. They even have a drink each. So they went to the bar, presumably one ordered for his mate, and they kept those honking great headphones on while ordering? Then they had the outright cheek to sit in front of Courtney Pine (slumming it as gigs go) wearing headphones listening to their old man music (Probably Status Quo or Genesis) while he blows straight.

Seems a bit unlikely doesn't it?

The Many Ultimate Defences for Gallifrey

Validium, the Doctor tells us (whoever the hell *he* is) was created as 'The ultimate defence for Gallifrey', they having presumably ditched the old transduction barrier when they realised someone could switch it off on a whim.

Validium was returned to Gallifrey at the end of this story so why didn't they use it during the Time War? It was after all the *ultimate* defence. So the Rose jack-in-a-box that John Hurt was pratting about with wasn't actually the final weapon he could've used? Why didn't they launch Nemesis at the Daleks?

Well as you can imagine, we have some theories.

Nemesis' form depends on the user, in this case Lady Peinforte, who chose to make a copy of herself and a bow and arrow. We have to assume that, since the bow and arrow are required in order to activate Nemesis, that this is a safeguard against misuse.

It must always be in three or more pieces. This doesn't make a lot of sense since the person using Nemesis decides on its shape. How did Lady Peinforte lose the bow in the first place? And what was this chunk of Validium doing on Earth? Did the Time Lords send it there to blow us all up? Maybe it was their first attempt at the whole thingy whatsit they used on Ravalox? We forget what it's called – Magnotron was it? Or was that the thing in *The Moonbase*? Well, whatever.

So Lady Peinforte decides it'll be a statue holding a bow and arrow, but who decides which two pieces are removable? It's just as possible that someone could've made off with the statue's knickers and eyeballs. That would've put a different spin on De Flore's display case. A big silver pair of Elizabethan fanny wrappers sitting on his desk.

The statue itself can move, so we have to assume since it's living metal, it can all move. So why couldn't the bow and arrow sprout little legs and run back to the statue? Instead they just glow a bit when they're pointing in the general direction. But hang on, the Doctor holds up the bow and it flashes a little bit, he turns around and it flashes more rapidly. But the bow *hasn't moved*. It's merely rotated. It's no nearer the statue than it was before. Bit odd. It's probably some sort of Time Lord thing we don't know about.

Validium really is the cat's tits. It decimates a whole fleet of Cyber warships. So returning again to the Time War, why didn't the Time Lords use it against the Daleks? And surely it's easy to make more Validium? It is after all just a metal. Even if it were a precious metal, if one statue shaped like a syphilitic old bat can knock out *thousands* of Cyber warships, surely it could've made mincemeat out of all those Dalek ships converging on Gallifrey in *Day of the Doctor* or *Night of the Doctor* or *Supper Time of the Doctor*? Whatever the hell it was called.

Is there a limit to the size of the chosen form for Nemesis? Could you say: 'Okay, Nemesis. I choose the shape of a whole planet' or 'Nemesis, be a mouse.' – maybe it's specific to a person-shape? In which case, why does it matter what shape Nemesis is? This seems like a special feature too many for such a unique item. Almost as daft as a weapon which is shaped like Rose Tyle... oh wait.

Sign Languish

The sign saying 'STAY IN YOUR CAR! WHILE IN THE SAFARI PARK' seems to be located quite some way inside the safari park, and on the wrong side of the road for car drivers to be able to see. Who is supposed to read this sign – the llamas? *Because the sign is facing the grass where the animals live.* Llamas don't drive cars so we don't know who this sign is intended for. Speaking of signs, Richard's gravestone appears to be in remarkably good condition considering that it is 331 years old and made of sandstone. It is almost as if the lettering has only just been carved given the lack of weathering on it. We've been to a graveyard and some of the headstones are in an appalling state – most of the time you can't see any of the lettering on them. Sandstone is particularly prone to erosion when exposed to the elements, so Richard has been very lucky here.

Going back to that wording on the sign, wouldn't it work better the other way around? In fact is the latter part even necessary since the sign is already in the safari park? Supermarkets don't have a sign that says 'Cash only at this till, inside this supermarket' do they? That chavvy fat-pit you have lunch in every day, McDonalds or 'the golden arches' as you probably call it, they don't say 'Would you like fries with the food you've just ordered or would you like them with something from the pizza place down the road?' – some things just don't need to be said. Yet again, an example of a sign-writer charging more per character than he needs to. Thieving sodbag.

The Brigadier's Day Out

The Doctor's friend the Brigadier is in this story. Yes he is because you can see the back of his head in the scene where he is being shown around 'Windsor Castle' – he's the one wearing the cap. We think that he must have gone the idea after visiting the café in which Lady Peinforte and Richard find themselves as there is a poster ton the wall there advertising 'Guided Tours of Royal Windsor'. What isn't known is that the visit to the castle formed only part of a day trip that he went on without his wife. We've ascertained exactly what the Brig did for the rest of the day. After arrival the group first had a bit of an amble around Windsor High Street before heading to the castle for a tour. There was a break for lunch, before they headed first to Eton College for a look around and then finally, they went off to have a look at the Savill Garden in nearby Egham.

Given that the Brigadier is presumably recently married it is quite surprising that Doris did not accompany him on this beano. Did the Brigadier leave her at home, or was she simply a fervent anti-royalist who refused to accompany him to a royal residence? As we've seen from *Mawdryn Undead*, we know that Alistair is a fan of the Queen and her lot, so this day out would be right up his street. But if he and his wife have such diametrically opposed opinions on the subject of the monarchy then it is hard to see how they could ever have a settled future, as arguments would inevitably crop up over the subject. Perhaps to try and placate his furious wife the Brigadier may have chosen to buy her a present from the Windsor Castle gift shop, although he would be hard-pressed to find anything there that would be suitable for somebody with her attitude towards the monarch. It would just all be royal-branded tea towels, thimbles and place mats.

It was of course Doris's choice not to go with her husband, but we can't imagine that she simply sat at home seething about things. We reckon that she doubtless got on with a bit of housework, did a bit of gardening and perhaps went down the shops to get something nice for tea. From what we see of her in *Battlefield*, she seems a perfectly pleasant sort of woman and there is no hint at all of a cleft between her and her husband. But mention the monarchy to her and you're in trouble.

We do hope that the Brigadier had a nice time on his trip, as he must be knackered from having to clean up Doris' massive lady's garden.

Fishy Gregorian

The entire plot of *Silver Nemesis* revolves around Lady Peinforte's bald mathematician accurately calculating the date of the Nemesis statue's return to Earth. As a number of commentators have pointed out, the introduction of the Gregorian calendar in the eighteenth century would have made this impossible without an eleven day slippage. The fact that the mathematician does correctly calculate the Nemesis' landfall without any knowledge of Gregorian time can only be resolved with a simple, yet dazzling conclusion, one that has significant repercussions across the rest of the series: *the Gregorian calendar was never adopted in the* **Doctor Who** *universe*. We have proof here that every date ever given in **Doctor Who** must be a Julian one. When De Flores arrives at the Nemesis crash site on 23rd November 1988, he's arriving in Julian time (a fortnight after the watching audience experiences that date). All those references in **Doctor Who** to events happening on 23rd November actually happened eleven days later than they appear to have done in our world. You're *literally* seeing into the future.

Now, we're not suggesting that this fully explains the vagaries of UNIT dating or the bright blue summer skies seen in the winters of *Remembrance of the Daleks* or *Silver Nemesis* (it's only eleven-or-so days) but it may explain why time sometimes seems strange, confused or made up in the **Doctor Who** universe.

Taking this idea to its logical extent, this means that any events in real history which are mentioned in the series and which occurred after the adoption of Gregorian time in Britain in 1752 also happened on different days. The Second World War that occurred in this Julian version of time happened eleven days late. The moon landing referred to in *The Impossible Astronaut / The Day of the Moon* (as we're required to call modern **Doctor Who** two-parters) took place half a month after it did in our world. Maybe the Cyberman invasion of the South Pole in December 1986 really *did* happen in our world, but everyone keeps missing all the evidence for it because they're searching in historical news broadcasts that are a fortnight out. Sort of like the Doctor Who Online news page.

Perhaps this tendency towards differing calendars in different universes extends further than we might otherwise assume. It could go some way towards explaining why the universe in *Inferno* is apparently operating at a different speed of time slightly ahead of ours: clearly in that parallel world, a different calendar was being employed, and the Inferno project that started on the 23rd of March (or whatever) in both worlds actually began a few days earlier in one of them. The same effect happens in *The Rise of the Cybermen* too: the TARDIS is clearly programmed for Gregorian dates and gets all confused when trying to land on the 14th of May in the Julian calendar (or whatever). How in *The Reign of Terror* it managed to get safely to the 22nd of Thermidor (or whatever) in the French Revolution is beyond us.

So how did this come about? Why does the **Doctor Who** universe operate on the principles of Julian time rather than our own Gregorian calendar? Well, it seems likely that the answer lies in the Doctor's meddling with time. The Doctor doesn't exist in our world so the calendar happened just as we remember, but in the **Doctor Who** universe, he does exist and presumably all his nipping back and forth through time has had a couple of unexpected consequences, one of which was Gregory XIII forgetting to introduce a revised dating system (or at least George II's later refusal to adopt that dirty continental calendar).

All this assumes the mathematician got his sums wrong. But maybe he got them right? Maybe this is the Time Lord Goronwy's final incarnation? Much like the Doctor's Valeyard, Goronwy's final mucked up incarnation travelled time and space in a bee hive bringing chaos and destruction to all. It was Goronwy who left Nemesis in Lady Peinforte's back garden (all euphemisms).

Either that, or just blame the chess set in Lady Peinforte's study like we do.

Unvention

One of the incongruities of this story is the fact that whilst the Doctor pimps up Ace's ghetto blaster to super-duper proportions he fails to do similar with its method of playing music. It still uses cassettes, for goodness sake. Cassettes (or tapes, as we called them) were just rubbish. They were always getting mangled up in the player, or would snap when being played so why on earth didn't the Doctor take the opportunity to improve on this design flaw? Had he not even considered the USB port? Or at a push, the compact disc? What kind of improvement has he actually made if the music is still being played via a stinky old tape? He included a space tracker transmitter and that globe hologram generating thing, but neglected to add a CD player. Perhaps tapes are all that Ace has with her given that she departed Ice World in a hurry, but you would have thought that the Doctor could have converted them to a more stable format if he was prepared to go to the extent of creating a fantastic new device to play them on. He's managed to improve his pocket watch by adding a digital display. Perhaps he just doesn't really care about Ace?

The Nemesis statue's impact on history:

1813: Pride & Prejudice is published

1838: Queen Victoria is crowned

1863: The American Civil War

1888: Jack the Ripper

1913: The eve of WW1 (that's a bit tenuous, but we reckon the Doctor was just winging that one)

1938: Hitler annexes Austria

1963: Kennedy assassinated

1988: A group of German tourists destroy and ultimately force the temporary two day closure of Windsor Safari Park

2013: **An Adventure in Time and Space** doesn't get a UK Blu-ray release.

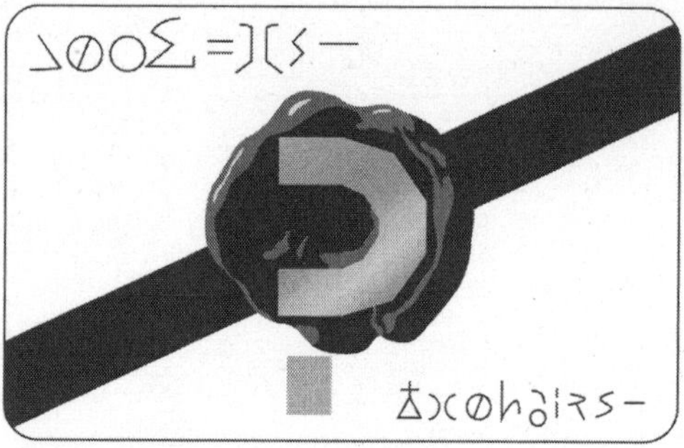

25d – *The Greatest Show in the Galaxy*

'Do you want me to do something 'orrible to your ears?'

Having received some junk mail, the Doctor and Ace travel to Segonax to see the legendary Psychic Circus.

Mags returns from Tesco with two bags of **Moonlighting** *DVDs and* **Twilight** *books.*

Come to Segonax…

Why wouldn't you come to Segonax? It's got a circus and a fruit and veg stall. Let's not even pack bags, we'll just skip and sing all the way there.

'Come to Segonax and visit the Psychic Circus!' declares the little robot. Those are all the directions you're getting.

Imagine for a moment that you're not a supercool **Doctor Who** fan with white hot fashion sense, a full head of hair and more notches on your bed post than Chancellor Flavia. You don't have two arms, two legs, a winky (or a lady-winky) and some eyes. Instead you're like a really big sausage with three heads, wings, gills and hand-hats. You breathe fire, cry acid and poo out shellfish - you're a spooky alien and you're unfamiliar with the world or indeed the universe. One day a postcard plops through the letterbox that says 'Come to Madame Tussaud's, the greatest waxworks in the galaxy. On Earth'. Just that. No other information, no postcode, country, satnav directions or even a local tube station.

It's not great advertising is it? It's no better than a drunken rumour. We're told the Psychic Circus lost its magic, but what it actually did was choose a bad marketing manager. We can assume, since she doesn't display any circus skills, that this marketing manager was Flower Child, especially since her face is on the side of their shitty old bus with the slogan 'The road is open and the rides are free'. Well you won't make any money that way, you dozy tart. That's like having a circus with free tickets. Just plain daft.

Presumably Flower Child joined them following her successful stint as head of tourism on Segonax. This is a planet with apparently very little going for it. The only local interest is a honking great circus. So why have they built their transmat pad thing 'miles and miles' from said circus? There's a huge advertising sign by the pad but no one thought to draw a little directional arrow on the bloody thing. Not so much as a 'You are here' map. Though in fairness it may as well be a piece of old sandpaper with a cross drawn on it.

Another of Segonax's failings is its lack of gift shop. The stallslady clearly got the contract somehow but what did she do to deserve it? One can theorise quite reasonably that it was some form of circus nepotism. Is it possible that the stallslady was Flower Child's predecessor? If so maybe she's either Juniper Berry or Peace Pipe? Both names imply a murky derivation. She's pretty cross so let's assume she's not Peace Pipe. But is she cross because she saw her once great circus ruined by the Psychic Yoko that is Flower Child? Most likely.

Pass the Remote

What do you notice when you look at your TV remote control? The sleek angles? Well, not if you have a Sony remote, those are shit. But most remotes have a lot of buttons, certainly more than two. And what do you notice about the remote control unit for say a model car or a boat? It has more than two buttons doesn't it?

Robot-building genius Bellboy has developed a magnificent feat of engineering in the remote control device he gives to Ace. This tiny box with its two buttons can perform a remarkable number of tasks. On, off, sit up, lay down, make noise like Stephen Hawking burping, shoot lasers at faces, shoot different laser at Chief Clown face, shoot chair leg… the combinations are endless.

More unusual is that this is clearly a very sophisticated remote control, presumably working from swipes and gestures across the two buttons. But none of this is explained to Ace when he gives her the box, she just instinctively knows how to work it. She's from the BBC Micro age. She's an idiot. She can't operate something that amazing.

It's almost as if the remote control is just an on-off switch for the robot.

Which begs a very different question: What purpose does this honking great laser bolt-firing robot serve in a circus? Which act used it? The clowns? Was it meant to fire water from its face and Bellboy used the wrong circuit board or something? Maybe it held a high-wire in its teeth and the lasers were there to, we don't know, make fireworks? No, that doesn't work. It'd burn the tent down. In fact, those lasers would be a huge fire-risk in such a tiny tent. Better pad it out with asbestos.

There's a further, more likely possibility, and that is that Bellboy was a pillock who couldn't design anything useful if his life depended on it which ironically it did in the end.

Let You Entertain Us

In *The Greatest Show in the Galaxy* the baddies are, as we know, The Gods of Ragnarok whose sole purpose is to be entertained by unwilling performers who are inevitably sent to their doom having failed to amuse the Gods. There are so many types of excellent entertainment that you have to wonder why on earth the Gods picked a circus as their choice of amusement. Circuses have never really been that great, and ones without any fierce animals even less so. The Psychic Circus is most definitely not 'The Greatest Show in the Galaxy', so just what was it that attracted them to it? It makes you wonder what other forms of entertainment they had presented to them before. Were they fans of all-in wrestling? Or did they go to a football match? Perhaps they set up some sort of talent show affair like **Opportunity Knocks**? We like the idea of a dolphin show at an aquarium. Stock car racing would have been impressive, as it would have added an element of true danger for the participants, but a circus? No, a circus is no good at all and we rather suspect that they only ended up there after their child pressured the parent gods into it:

Child God:	Mother, father, can we do a circus this time? Can we? Can we?
Mother God:	Don't be so silly, circuses are rubbish.
Child God:	Pleeeassseee.
Father God:	It's a fair suggestion Mother; we've never done a circus before.
Mother God:	I'd rather not Father. Although I do quite fancy the idea of a prize marrow contest or something like that. You know, like in a village show. They have jam and cakes at those.
Child:	Eh?
Father God:	How on earth would that be in any way entertaining Mother? What a ridiculous suggestion. No, I say we do a circus as Child God suggests. I'd quite like to see a bunch of lions going rampant and tearing some clowns apart.
Child:	Go on, go on!
Mother God:	Oh, alright then… If we must… But next time, *I* get to choose and it won't be anything as ghastly and dull as a circus.

That's probably how the Gods found themselves in a big top watching the Doctor do his Great Soprendo act. The animal element could probably have been accommodated had the Doctor done all that business with the ferrets, but, as we know ferrets aren't traditionally a circus act.

Maybe the Gods should've signed up for Nostalgia Tours? Those are entertaining as hell. Or is there the slimmest chance that the Gods rule the The War Lord and his people? Were those war games for the benefit of the Gods of Ragnarok?

The Psychic Circus seems an incredibly drab form of entertainment for the Gods. Why exactly did they pick this one as their latest form of amusement? Was it something to do with the psychic element that attracted them, or was that merely an added bonus on top of the clowns? Where had this circus been before it arrived on Segonax and how did the Gods get to hear about it? It's possible that they got one of those advertising robots that materialised in the Doctor's TARDIS and Child God got all excited.

As circuses go, this one seems to be rather tiny in size, so scale can't have been a factor that attracted the Gods. If it was the 'Most Hugest Circus in the Galaxy' then that would have been really quite something. Look at the size of the ring – it's *miniscule* for a circus. If the circus did feature animals then this ring could probably only manage to accommodate a few hamsters or possibly a small dog at most. The majority of folk visiting a circus would prefer to see a massive ring, but for some reason the Gods are satisfied with this petite, dainty one. If there is one thing that you want to see when you go to the circus then it's a vast, inviting ring.

Anyway, they've got it easy. What about the God who wore black and red make-up and went rogue? You know, the same bored eternal sitting in a chair doing nothing: Sutekh. Look at him. Same pose, same lack of tolerance for fannying about – he's the fourth God of Ragnarok.

The TARDIS

There are races out there that would trade several of their appendages for the ability to be able to just beam aboard the TARDIS unmolested. Daleks, Cybermen, Sontarans, they've all tried to gain access to the supposedly impregnable time machine. If only they'd known that a spam bot was the key to unlimited access. That said the Doctor seems remarkably unfazed by the sudden appearance. Certainly, some of that must be due to the fact that he was pratting about in a circusy type way at the time, so the spam was at least relevant. But take a step back, Time Lord and look at the bigger picture – your TARDIS was invaded by a foreign body with consummate ease. It then took control of your communication system. Is that not a cause for alarm?

We're constantly in a state of outrage at some of the unwanted mail that pops into our mailboxes with relentless regularity. Apart from the ones about penis enlargement – there's one of the Auton team who are more than interested in maximising their member, so there's a special mailbox for those at Auton Towers. But spam, generally, is a bad thing. Spam in the future, given that it evidently still exists, must be an absolute nightmare. But the kind of spam that has a physical presence, that you can touch and feel and if you've any sense, kick very hard against a wall, is an alarming development.

Strange that others haven't made use of this spam. Kane for example could promote Iceworld with it, Goronwy could sell honey, Vorg could sell the miniscope and Mergrave could sell his jollop.

More appropriately the Shit Weapons Daleks could've made use of these spam bots during the Time War.

Up Among the Gods

The hidden overlords of the Psychic Circus are basically bored elementals out for a good time. And of course there's absolutely nothing wrong with that. But there's a lot more going on in the universe to distract and amuse than sitting in a dusty old tent, scavenging on the occasional poor sap who wanders by. If only they'd get out once in a while they'd probably be a lot happier and the likes of Whizz Kid and dear old Nord could have gone about their business unmolested (It's our 'word of the week').

The scheme of appearing in the real universe as a bored 1950s family is one way of mainlining what little psychic juice there is, but we're forced to wonder how they get to choose who's playing who. Are they locked into their role? If so, how does the one playing the little girl feel about it? It's not very god-like to be denied an ice cream by one's peers and simply sit there and take it like a petulant child. Of the three, it's really only the father figure who can honestly be seen to be getting the best out of the deal. As paterfamilias, he's afforded the responsibility and dignity of being the one in charge, whereas the other two are subject to his whims.

This opens up a world of possibilities which might go some way towards explaining the nature of the Gods of Ragnarok. There's a sense that dressing up as a middle-aged woman and a child are just the kind of quirks that two of them enjoy. So, if a transvestite showed up at the circus looking for a good time, presumably they'd be okay, at least for a bit, given that they're, for want of a better phrase, preaching to the audience. Of course, this same theory means that the peccadilloes of the middle one are best left unexamined.

When we finally meet the Gods in the flesh (or is it stone? If it is, then it's a surprisingly malleable kind of stone – it's probably just grey painted foam, knowing those old frauds) it has to be said they're a lot more threatening than the bored looking family in the big top. This is probably for the best, as nobody's going to be at the top of their game, performance wise, if they knew they were being sat in judgement upon by anything that looked like that. Then again, the implied threat of the Gods' true form would instil a certain urgency on the part of the performer. Not that the Doctor seems particularly worried. He has, as always, got something up his sleeve. In this case a bouquet of magician's flowers and, had they given him enough time to complete his act, a rubber chicken and one of those things that fires playing cards really, really fast.

M-O-O-N

Werewolves transform when they see the moon, as everyone well knows. Mags, on the other hand is a special breed of werewolf who transforms at the merest sight of something moon related, in this case a stage light in the shape of a crescent moon. Now, your common or garden werewolf is a dangerous beast, to be sure, but Mags and her race take that danger to a whole new level. Presumably any pictorial representation would set her off. So that's sitting down for a chuckle with the kids at the antics of **The Clangers** well and truly out of the question. **Button Moon**, too. Mags won't be following Mr Spoon, for which she has our sympathies. Just how far does this lunacy (in the most literal sense of the word) extend? Does the word 'moon' either written or spoken set her off, for example? Is Mags forever denied the liquid smooth tones of Andy Williams singing *Moon River* or the popular 1990s detective drama **Moon and Son**? Actually, in the case of the latter it's probably for the best, as it really wasn't up to much to be brutally honest. Millicent Martin is an amazing performer but **Moon and Son** was badly thought out and hopelessly predictable. Actually, speaking of Millicent Martin, what about her role in **Frasier** as the mother of housekeeper, Daphne Moon? The cultural limitations of such a condition are staggering. A life without Clangers or snuggling up on the sofa to watch **Breakfast at Tiffany's**? No, that's too much to bear.

The Psychic Circus

It has to be said there's not a great deal of evidence that the acts or indeed the customer-facing premise of the Psychic Circus are particularly, you know, psychic. They have psychic spam (assuming the little spam bot knew the Doctor was juggling at the point of insertion), but otherwise the only evidence of any kind of ESP seems to be the bad guys sapping the life out of the poor idiots that decide to visit. And that's really not the kind of psychic you want to put on your posters. Perhaps, then, they're the victim of a particularly inept or creatively insistent sign-writer?

'Mr Bellboy, are you sure you really want "Psychotic Circus"? You're paying by the letter, you know and I have to say it doesn't sound all that enticing to me. Tell you what, why not just go with "Psychic Circus"? It's got more of a ring to it, plus you're saving a few quid on cost'.

We don't know about you, but if we stumped up our hard-earned cash for tickets to something called a Psychic Circus, we'd be pretty miffed if all that was on offer was a few half-hearted clowns and a rapper who's clearly had enough. Worse still, to then discover that we were, in fact, the main act would be the icing on a decidedly mouldy-looking cake. Not that we'd be worried, of course, we'd wow those miserable Gods and probably go on to become the star attraction or something. No wonder they stopped charging for tickets.

Now, at least if they were up front about it and sent out flyers to the Psychotic Circus, we'd not be alone in thinking 'bloody hell – that sounds interesting! I wonder what's so psychotic about it? Bet it's really dangerous stuff' and thus our interest would be well and truly piqued. Of course, we'd only have ourselves to blame for anything that happened once we'd gone into the big top, but there'd be no danger of any complaints about false advertising, that's for sure.

Those clowns wandering about the place in their hearse aren't exactly the best advertisement either. It's a well-established fact (probably) that most people find clowns creepy rather than hilarious, so they're probably doing more harm than good by driving around the countryside looking all sinister. Yes, we know they *are* sinister, but surely the whole point of the circus is to get punters through the door (or in this case, flaps). The ultimate fate (and it really is the ultimate fate) of those punters is irrelevant from a sales and marketing perspective; you want to draw a crowd. No matter how you look at it, the Psychic Circus is a disaster. The acts are rubbish, the advertising would put any sane individual off getting within a light year of the place and they appear to have pitched up on one of the least populated planets in the galaxy they claim to be the greatest show in.

Presumably, those who come to try out for the circus themselves have been similarly spammed by those horrible little junk mail robots. Can you honestly see Nord being challenged by the spiteful little dustbin? He'd stamp it into the ground! Whizz Kid wouldn't need much persuading because he's already their biggest fan, but fan of what? If the circus really was so well celebrated the buzz about the place must have taken a downturn round about the time audiences stopped returning from a night out.

Season 26

It all concluded in 1989.

The Berlin Wall comes down, thanks to David Hasselhoff, Ted Bundy is executed (pretty sure Hasselhoff wasn't involved), The Tiananmen Square protests rock China, the Hillsborough disaster claims the lives of 96 football fans, the Dalai Llama wins the Nobel Peace Prize, Daniel Radcliffe, The Sega Genesis and Taylor Swift are born, we sadly lose Joe Spinell, Sergio Leone and Graham Chapman and **Indiana Jones and the Last Crusade** tops the US box office.

Meanwhile in Carbury…

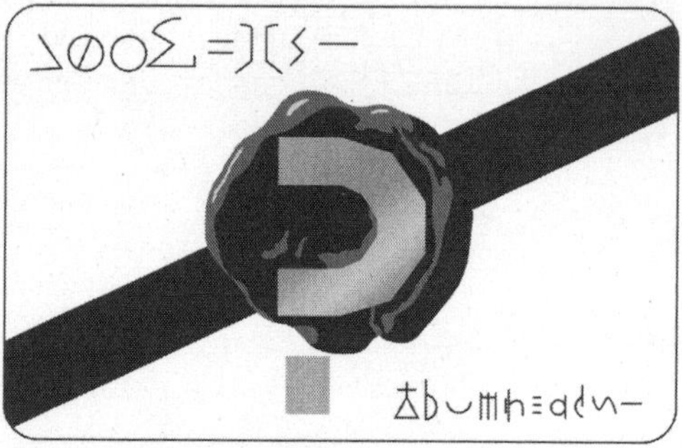

26a – *Battlefield*

> *'BOOOOOOOOOOMMMM!'*

Well… there are these knights, a witch, and an archaeologist, and the Brigadier (two Brigadiers) and a Destroyer and Bessie and a hot Czech chopper pilot… so good she's worth mentioning twice.

Benton done a tree bad.

'Sergeant Benton, tree planting party, at the double!'

It's a testament to Sergeant Benton's loyalty and capability as a member of The Brigadier's squad that even now, 15/25 years later, depending on the dating protocol, he's the first person who springs to mind when there's a tree to stick in the ground. But then Sergeant Benton was always something of a favourite. His unswerving loyalty to his superior officers and willingness to muck in and be the first to volunteer whenever danger was at hand endeared him to his fellow UNIT colleagues. He was like a big, affectionate puppy – not too much going on upstairs but always happy to put himself out there should the occasion arise. Last seen by the Brigadier selling second hand cars, it's sad to think that just 4 short years later Benton was electrocuted at a UNIT reunion when a careless waiter tripped and upended a carafe of Paul Mason all over him while he was eulogising at the microphone about his glory days. Sadder still was the fact that for the first few seconds the assembled audience thought it was part of his act and that he was simply acting out rather too enthusiastically one of his escapades from back in the day. Poor, unfortunate, hapless Benton.

As to which tree Benton would be best at planting, well we just can't be sure. No two saplings are the same (unless they're so similar as to be identical). Our investigations led us to a top secret UNIT file labelled 'Operation Yew Tree'. Make an 'orse sick, that would.

Eater of Worlds, Nibbler of Moons

When asked what he wants to do with the Earth, the Destroyer responds 'Devour it' – or words to that effect. We're nit-pickers but we have our own boundaries and we're not winding back and forth through the DVD just to find the one line. Do it yourself. If you're going to be that pedantic then you're probably grimacing at the phrase 'winding back and forth' which wouldn't apply to a DVD, only a videotape.

The point is – he is repeatedly stated to eat worlds, devour them, gobble them up etc.

Let's consider the mechanics of this. The Destroyer is roughly the same height as say, Chris Tarrant or maybe David Hasselhoff. He has dreadlocks, a tail and a blue pot belly; but that's a very small belly.

Let's run with the idea that, since he's a god of some sort or at the very least a demon, he's got a transcendentally dimensional tummy. Where does one begin when devouring a world? Right now he's in an old church in England. Eating England will take some time and when he's done that he's got one almighty drink ahead of him before he finds the next land mass. This is good as it'll wash down the things he's eaten which include a few million TV sets, several thousand miles of tarmac, at least twenty pillows, some bicycles, some cars, lots and lots of dirt and many, many eggs. He's got to devour everything, including the Earth's core which is really, really hot. (We know, we looked it up in a book. He'll have to eat that book too. And us. And this book you're reading now. All ten copies of it).

Now we're no nutrition experts, but we've seen enough episodes of **Man vs Food** to know that such a feast shouldn't be undertaken lightly. You need a method and a process in order to tackle what is essentially a food mountain. The Destroyer, we must assume, is an experienced hand at this and knows what he's doing. He'll have a plan in place. He'll know to save something as a dipping sauce towards the end, a tart condiment to get those last few drops down. Maybe that's what the Earth's molten core of magma is for? Sweet chilli dip.

This is all well and good, but if we go back to the Destroyer's size for a moment, and the aforementioned oceans that need drinking we have to discuss something that we here at **Auton** don't like to talk about often: the toilet. How do you poo out a world as you eat it? Surely if you stockpile up your own Worldpoos then eventually you have to eat those too since they've become a part of the world you're eating. It's possible, since we've not seen him in action, that the Destroyer is capable of crouching on the ground, blue bum raised in the air, and firing flipping great balls of arse-debris out into space. This is acceptable, but what of his honking great Destroyer bladder? Maybe this is how he cools the Earth's core? Wee on it first, then it's cooled down enough to use as a dip.

Good Destroyer tooth hygiene is essential. If he chips a tooth on Paris or a hubcap or Tom Jones or something, then he's going to be severely disabled regards his primary function (the eating of worlds). He presumably takes a nap during the devouring process so must have to floss, brush and freshen each day.

If we return to the **Man vs Food** scenario it's also possible that at the end of each world, if he manages it, there's a prize to be won – be it a t-shirt, an electric guitar or virgin or something. Maybe the other gods and demons gather around and cheer him on like rednecks in a burger bar? Azal in the corner screaming: 'You can do it, The Destroyer, Eater of Worlds. Eat that world, baby! Eat that world, baby!' while Sutekh the Destroyer (any relation?) sits to one side quietly willing him to succeed. Elsewhere Omega is air punching and whooping like a hyperactive toddler asked to impersonate a runaway train.

To have the name 'The Destroyer, Eater of Worlds' he must have form. It's not a label you can give yourself lightly. Mind you, it could all be bluster and something he added to his Demon C.V. to impress Morgaine when he applied for the job. She seems pretty gullible. He never thought she'd actually release him and expect him to do the job. This is why, when released, he doesn't immediately start licking the wall like a starved lunatic.

How long was he chained up for anyway? Those chains are all well and good, but shouldn't he be wearing some sort of Hannibal Lecter mask to stop him eating worlds? He could do a lot of damage if left unchecked. But similarly Morgaine values him as a pawn in her game so must presumably have to keep him fed while chained. Does this mean there's a Destroyer feeding time? Morgaine straps him into a high chair and does the choo-choo train with a fork full of kippers? It seems unlikely, and how do you feed an Eater of Worlds from a fork? The fork is part of the world so he'll eat it, just as he'd eat a plate, a table and a chair and the person supplying the fork, plate, table and chair.

Was the Destroyer born to eat worlds or did he train himself up? At what point in life did he realise he had a talent for eating worlds? It's not a talent you happen upon by chance. This whole Eater of Worlds thing simply doesn't work. It was clearly a buffed C.V.

Where does the Destroyer even come from? It's implied that Ace and Shou Youing could be taken to be his 'handmaidens in Hell-hur-hur-hur-hur', which implies a Christian society drives these aliens. Christianity didn't really come to England proper until after Arthur's time (the death of Penda in 655 was the big change) so Morgaine was probably using Hades as a threat before Poppa Augustine brought her people The Church. The Destroyer must've spent years in the early days just terrorising Palestine.

By the way, Hell doesn't sound too bad if you get handmaidens when you go there, unless they're the sort of handmaidens who will be dressing the Destroyer up in flowery velvet dresses and undoing his corset and suchlike.

Phwoar.

UNIT dating

UNIT is a top secret organisation. This love of secrecy is made clear by the fact that, as we see in episode one, Brigadier Bambera has no knowledge of the Doctor and his ability to change his appearance and Zbrigniev does. Zbrigniev was there in the 1970s (or possibly, as we say, the 1980s) working alongside Lethbridge-Stewart and so knows of the Doctor from personal experience. Bambera, who wasn't, doesn't.

The fact that it's just the Brigadier, Zbrigniev and possibly Mike Yates (although *Dimensions in Time* didn't make it clear whether that *was* Mike Yates or not – it could have and indeed most likely was one of the Rani's projections – just like Bessie – and, come to think of it like the gun Yates fired at the Rani…hell, just when we thought we understood that one) are the only survivors of UNIT's glory days of the 1970s (or possibly, as we say, the 1980s) means that there's precious little accurate knowledge of UNIT operations, protocols or HR records for those joining the modern UNIT of the 1990s (or possibly 2000s). They are, in many ways, learning everything afresh with each operation, which would go some way towards explaining why nobody recognises an electromagnetic pulse or that the most common cause of such an event would be some kind of nuclear event, caused by, oh we don't know, maybe the

sodding great rocket you're carting about the countryside.
The old adage 'old soldiers never die…' was never more true than in the case of UNIT. They try to keep their distinguished service men and women around for as long as they possibly can because it's the only way they can be sure that what they're doing isn't going to end up getting them killed.

There's no substitute for experience, particularly when your filing system is based on nothing more sophisticated than shared memories. When we next meet Lethbridge-Stewart (or at least the Lethbridge-Stewart we can be sure isn't conjured up by the Rani) he's whiling his final days away in a nursing home where, fuelled by scotch, he spends every waking hour telling UNIT recruits over and over again the story of the Doctor, previous UNIT operations, where the keys to the motor pool are kept and what an enormous idiot Benton was and how he completely fouled up Operation Yew Tree.

In *Battlefield*, we see the Brigadier brought back in to service because he's the only one in the whole organisation who knows the truth about the Doctor and because he knows where the spare batteries for the convoy are kept. But what use do they think the Brigadier will actually be? Actually, what use is he in the long run? If anything he complicates matters for the Doctor who'd have managed just fine without him. Except possibly the 3D snake thing. But anyone could've done that and made it go BOOOOOOOOOOOOOOOOOM!!!

Intergalactic Plastic Knights

Ancelyn, Mordred, good knights and bad; it's a miracle any of them make it to Earth in one piece given that they fly headlong through the vortex and plummet head-first into the ground without even the most rudimentary attempt at a landing manoeuvre – then explode. As space travel goes, the space knights of Space Camelot have devised a unique method which both helps keep their numbers down to a manageable dozen or so at most at any given time and which strikes mortal terror into any who come into contact with them. The thinking being 'JESUS CHRIST – did you see that?! That mad bastard just flew headfirst into a building, exploded and then came at me with a sword!'

The legendary Knights of the Round Space Table are legendary because of their valour, their chivalry and above all their immense reputation for being double-hard bastards. Not just anyone can dive from planetary orbit into the ground and walk away in one piece, let alone launch into a spirited defence of the realm, clad only in a suit of plastic armour and a winning smile. To make themselves even more awesome, each knight must perfect the ability to rouse themselves from whichever crater or wall they've embedded themselves in and emerge in an altogether unnerving motion which makes it look like they're floating out of the very earth. These guys *really* know how to make an entrance.

The On-going Crassness of Ace

When Bambera finally introduces herself properly to the Doctor and Ace, she reveals her full name to be 'Winifred Bambera'. Ace's incredulous cry of 'Winifred' is not only so downright bloody rude that she's lucky the SheBrig doesn't give her a slap, it's also further evidence of just how moronic the girl continues to be. For the past two years she's been travelling all over the universe with the Doctor. She's met Daleks, Cybermen, seen empires rise and fall, planets which are really spaceships and all manner of strange and wonderful things. Yet she's amazed to the point of outburst by the name 'Winifred'. Idiot.

As for 'BOOOOOOOOM', there is a moment there where even the Doctor's chivalrous avoidance of hurting a woman would be put to the test. We've physically destroyed two television sets and chewed through a DVD because of that one scene.

The Happy Couple

As is hinted at during the course of this story, Ancelyn and Bambera seem to be getting on well and look set to make a go of things. Now, this leads us to wonder how a knight from years ago would manage to adapt to the modern world. Ancelyn comes from long ago and things in the present day would surely baffle him? He'd have to find some way of earning a living, so what would he do for a job? Is there any call in 20th century Britain for a sword-wielding soldier like him? The Brigadier asks him if he is any good with a lawn mower, but he fails to answer so it looks as though gardening would be out of the question. So what work would be available for Ancelyn and where would his limited range of skills lead him? Well he's good with a sword so he might be useful as sous chef in a restaurant, chopping up onions and carrots and the like and he is quite agile so could probably be some sort of P.E. teacher. Unless he chose to become a Robin Hood impersonator in Nottingham then there really isn't a worthwhile, productive role that he could fulfil and so he should be sent back to his own time. Or dimension. Or whatever.

In some of the spin-off novels that followed the TV series we discover that Ancelyn and Bambera get married and have children, but somehow we just can't imagine him as a househusband – he'd be just hopeless. He wouldn't know how to work an oven, would probably be scared of a vacuum cleaner, thinking it the work of the devil! He'd definitely struggle with wallpapering the front room. Would he even know how to work a modern toilet, or would he simply dig a hole in the garden and do his business there?

A pairing across the ages such as the one between these two would invariably be fraught with difficulty. Who knows which filthy historical pox Ancelyn might be saddled with? Would he inform his intended if he did have something nasty, indeed would he even know if he was infected? He could have a disease for which there is no known cure and poor Winifred may end up ridden with pustulating boils or an infected portion of her body.

Suppose that everything was fine on the health front and Ancelyn and Bambera were able to go ahead with their nuptials. Ancelyn is making most of the play between the two of them in the story, so we would imagine that it would be him who would propose to her, but he wouldn't have an engagement ring to give her unless he could manage to fashion one from part of his armour. Would they have had stag and hen parties? We'd imagine that the stag party would be a pretty raucous affair with nasty games with swords and knives, and given that Bambera is in the army then that would probably have been fairly boisterous too. The problem for Ancelyn is that he doesn't know anybody in this time, so who exactly would he invite to his party? He can hardly get on the blower to Gawain or Sir Percival can he? We picture Ancelyn and the Brigadier, together with Zbrigniev and Pat from the pub, sitting around, sipping Arthur's Ale while Pat's wife does her pole dance.

If the pair were to have children during their marriage then having a father from the time of King Arthur and a mother from the modern world would be quite hard on the kids. Imagine knowing that you had grandparents, but that they lived over a thousand years ago. The poor kids wouldn't be able to get birthday or Christmas cards or even visit them without the help of the Doctor and the TARDIS. And we bet that the poor children would get regularly mocked at school for having a dad who brushes his teeth with a twig and some salt.

Over Cautiousness

The Doctor has built a secret tunnel leading to Arthur's spaceship beneath Lake Vortigern. A tunnel which opens only on his voice print; a tunnel therefore that he's designed to lead to things and places that the Doctor, and only the Doctor can control. Apart, that is, from the security system. That is apparently keyed to an entirely different system that can only be overcome by randomly pressing buttons, leaping over stanchions and having someone wander in with the foresight to step on a flashing, painted egg carton. The ways of Merlin are impossible to fathom by us mere mortals.

We can only wonder just what it is the Doctor/Merlin was trying to protect with such an intricately planned security protocol. Clearly, it wasn't the sword Excalibur, which Ace managed to purloin with relative ease, thanks to a handy space torpedo tube. Nor was it Arthur, who lay dead on the ground, not sleeping as the legend would have us believe.

But then, as we've seen from the seventh Doctor's previous adventures, he only ever seems to come up with half a plan. Outwitted by the renegade shit-Dalek faction in *Remembrance of the Daleks* and outfoxed by the Cybermen in *Silver Nemesis*, this darker, more powerful Doctor is no less a bungling idiot than any of his more frivolous predecessors; he simply manages to look more capable by lowering his voice and speaking in a commanding voice whenever anyone rumbles him.

Think about it: the Doctor is one of a select few individuals floating about the place that possess a machine that can simply materialise wherever it needs to go. So the tunnel is, by its very nature, superfluous. If he really wanted to get down there he could just pop aboard the TARDIS.

Then there's the 'voice print' activated door. Any mobile phone with a recording capability (ie. All of them) would have you through that before you could say 'poltrrrrroon', or, failing that, a half-decent impersonator who could put on a convincing Scottish accent.

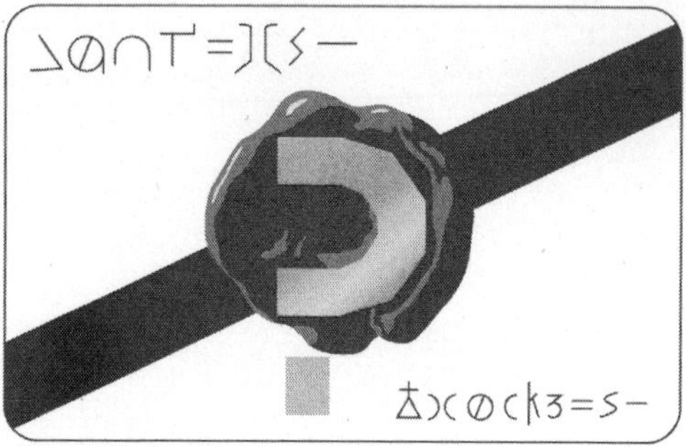

26b – *Ghost Light*

'Of course, if she were a real lady, I wouldn't be in her boudoir'

Attempting to survey all organic life, a being named Light and his survey team run into the irritating complication of evolution.

Nimrod's Fang Gang

Light and Evolution

The plot of *Ghost Light* is such that Light may more properly be termed 'Argos'. He's a cataloguer of species, and the plot of *Ghost Light* essentially involves him getting upset at Argos' insistence on selling random action figures on a 'styles may vary' basis. He's upset that it hasn't been made exactly clear to him what he's getting. Alternatively, he can be considered a colleague of Captain Cook from *The Greatest Show in the Galaxy*, because they share the same job.

Light is a member of an advanced space-faring species with the power to manipulate matter by the process of thought, yet he isn't yet aware of the concept of evolution, something the story takes pains to clarify was a burgeoning realisation to even Victorian man. Where does Light think he himself came from? Or all of the creatures he surveys? The result of some omnipotent being? Spontaneously thrown up as a consequence of a sentient universe? The great Light-stork in the sky? We'd love to have a chat to him for half an hour on his insight into religion: it must be fascinating. We wonder what other technological and scientific developments Light's society totally missed out on? Although they appear to have invented matter teleportation, perhaps they've yet to invent the light bulb? Their ability to reanimate discarded skin-husks of the dead is extremely impressive, but the lack of a Dyson vacuum cleaner on Lightworld is bound to cause problems for the cleaners. And as for their ability to kill another life form with only a glance? Well, it's very good, but given the choice we'd much prefer they had sliced bread.

How many planets do you think Light surveyed before he discovered the idea that organisms change as they grow? Perhaps that's why he's so upset at the end of the story: he's fully aware that he's going to have to go back to Aridius and

Megalophon and Skaro and do them again. That'd tax anyone's mind. Have you ever spent ages writing an essay in Word, or creating something wonderful in Photoshop, or editing some complex video footage together in an Avid suite, only to accidentally delete it all or save over it with another file? The thought of starting it all over again is terrifying. Imagine Light trying to come to terms with all the different Cybermen or Silurians with tits!

As it transpires, Light ultimately meets his downfall when he's confronted unexpectedly by the Doctor's Bandersnatch. In his attempts at cataloguing all life in the universe, he visits Earth with his survey team. Quite why he's doing all this is up for grabs, but his method is insane. Rather than looking at every creature that exists, he decides to send one creature (Josiah) out into the world to evolve its way up the food chain to become duplicates of every creature on the planet before settling on humans as the paragon of animals and killing Queen Victoria to become the paragon of humans. We've already established that the denouement of the story means that Light must be thoroughly unaware of the process of evolution for the climax to make any sense, and yet Light's entire plan revolves around him being exactly aware of how evolution works because his survey module (Josiah) is required to evolve into the most complex life-form on the planet for the cataloguing process to work. Something doesn't quite add up here.

Of course, the process that the survey team goes through isn't how evolution works anyway, not even in the **Doctor Who Discovers** range of books (and we're assuming the Doctor wrote them, as it says so on the cover). If you've decided to evolve into a primate, you can't also evolve into a lizard or an insect or a whale or an echidna or a duck or whatever. How then is Light hoping to catalogue rabbits or pterodactyls or marmosets? I bet he'd love a hamster but he'll never see one.

Ditto sheep and baby hedgehogs. He'll only manage various creatures of the hominid line and their illustrious ancestors. Like Nimrod. As an aside, it's stated that Earthmen never invite their ancestors round to dinner, which seems a little insensitive given that they've got Nimrod serving the peas.

So what, then, are those husk things? Our grasp of evolutionary biology is not quite as copious or extreme as, say, Charles Darwin's, but we're pretty sure that human beings did not evolve from six-foot half-human insects or lizards, which those two husks seem to be. Why are they insectoid? Why are the lizardly? Why are they man-shaped? Why would Light's process create these beings? We have no idea. We're in the dark. If only we had a light bulb.

Josiah's Household

What exactly do they do all day? At 5.59pm, the day staff all clear out of there like the place is suddenly about to come over all evil and a minute later, at the stroke of six, Josiah and the rest of the inhuman household all come to life. So what are they made of? We know they're all elements of Light's experiment into evolution. But what part in that experiment do the housemaids serve? And what of Gwendoline? Josiah, as we know (or we should if we've been paying attention, come on, it's not that hard to comprehend) is the test subject, Control is the control subject. So, Gwendoline – presumably she's genetic stock for Josiah to get evolutionary on. Surely with Light's powers over creation he can convince a few menials to get over themselves and do a bit of overtime. After all, times were hard in Victorian days, so they could have surely used the extra money.

Josiah's Evil Lotion

The crypt below the house is full of Josiah's discarded bodies, but what of the rest of his evolutionary dead ends over the years? Look closely around the house and you'll see more of his discarded, yet strangely still animated, former selves:

> That rocking horse in the lab – that's him. Josiah's short-lived equine experiments were going nowhere, but he seemed to get a lot of action from young Gwendoline after he evolved a pair of runners and a welcoming demeanour.

> The stuffed and mounted animal heads that adorn the corridors – they're all former Josiahs too. Some of his most treasured husks are more than they appear. Josiah couldn't bring himself to behead the ocelot, the rhino and the lion and so those bodies remain intact, their heads poking through the wall in the upstairs corridor while the bodies stretch out into the rooms behind. Gwendolyn's bedroom has the back-end of the rhino obscuring her view of the picture window as it balances atop a walnut credenza. The lion takes up most of the second floor bathroom and the ocelot provides an amusing decorative light fixture in what was once Redvers' room.

> The bearskin rug in the sitting room is another of Josiah's cast-offs. Ursine life was one of his less pleasant experiments, thanks to a run-in with a trapper. Josiah narrowly escaped becoming a wall trophy for real while in this body, but his sense of irony enabled him to see the funny side. The trapper stands proud within a full grizzly skin in the conservatory while Josiah's own discarded remains make for a supremely comfortable rug.

Shine a Light

Light's affection for those within Gabriel Chase is fickle, of course. He operates on a different plane to those mere mortals. As an elemental of immense power, he thinks nothing of spending his days off in a cigarette case on the floor of Redvers' cell. It may look small and cramped to the likes of you and me but he's got it done up beautifully in there, between the Rizlas and the baccy.

When we finally meet Light incarnate during the third episode, note that he is not named simply for his illuminated clothing. Light is light in every conceivable way – notice the way he seems to tip-toe across the floor like a ballerina. Light, being composed entirely of light, has negligible mass and has not yet come to terms with the concept of gravity. Having miscalculated his corporeal form somewhat, he struggles to remain on the floor. Thus, his all-powerful appearance is diminished. Realising the effect this mistake has on his audience, he resorts to travelling at the speed of light and simply appearing in a flash when we next meet him. But too late. The Doctor has already made his mind up and treats his sudden materialisation as a mere parlour trick.

Light's voice is similarly affected in order to cement his overall appearance of lightness, but his attempt at a falsetto is amateurish at best.

Light is also Light Lite. Same as Light but with fewer calories. The Dapol Light Lite Night Light had two extra arms and was blue.

Tooth, the Whole Tooth and Nothing but the Tooth

When the Doctor hands Nimrod a bear's tooth, we're led to believe that it signifies the owner has great wisdom. Which is true, based on our extensive research into Neanderthal cave paintings. What Nimrod doesn't know, however, is that it was simply the first thing that came to hand when the Doctor reached into his pocket. It could just as easily been a mouldy jelly baby or a calling card for Fast Betty that the Doctor picked up in a London phone box and which he insists was simply the first piece of paper that was available when he overheard a villainous plot being hatched in a south London pub and needed to write down the salient points. Given the available space between Betty's particulars and crudely obscured photographs, the Doctor appears to have written the notes in his own unique shorthand; a series of stars, what appears to be the number 9 underlined three times and what to the casual observer looks like a mobile telephone number scrawled in extreme haste.

The bear tooth itself was one of a handful of trinkets the Doctor picked up at a market stall in Covent Garden, along with a rabbit's foot, a shark's tooth and the dried foreskin of a cat.

Interestingly, all three carry their own unique meanings in Neanderthal lore:

> A rabbit's foot is a signifier of good luck, then as now.
> A shark's tooth, worn around the neck, is intended to ward off danger. Danger, such as sharks violently paranoid about losing their teeth.
> The dried foreskin is thought to signify that the bearer is one of immense speed and agility. Unless it's the bearer's own foreskin in which case they've likely been hanging around in Dutch crypts.

Light Housework

Why do the maids wait in the wood panelling of the house? Just what was the wording on the advert for that job? 'Required – housemaids. Must be happy to hide in a cupboard all day, be able to shoot a pistol, and not bat an eyelid at serving soup made from people'?

Mrs Grose, the landlady, has an odd way of leaving rooms with the phrase 'after dark'. Was this also a condition of employment? Does she know there are maids in the walls? Do they dust them off during the day? Who washes the maids' uniforms? If they live in the wall then does this mean they have a wardrobe in the wall as well? This harks back to *Black Orchid* where servants were kept in cupboards, upside down with their necks broken. Both stories feature the actor Michael Cochrane so we're theorising this a contractual stipulation he has when appearing in **Doctor Who**.

Husk Crisps

How exactly do the husks come to life? We learn that they are the old skins of Josiah Smith, but why do they move about? This aspect of evolution is a similar fashion to that of a snake, but imagine if their cast-off skins could be animated like this – there'd be crispy snake and gecko ghosts slithering and crawling around the planet everywhere. Chaos would ensue and the council would have a dreadful time trying to control them and clean up the crunchy mess that they would deposit. Once the husks in Gabriel Chase are finally exhausted we should be told what happens to them. Can they be put out in the recycling bin, or do they have to go in with the normal rubbish? Would the local council accept husks as household waste and take them away with the bins along with the rest of the rubbish, or would

Josiah have had to arrange a special collection (for which a fee is usually levied)?

Perhaps the leftover husks are edible? It's a shame that Smith never considered this because British people love crisps and chopped-up husks could have made a very lucrative snack product for a Victorian population who had little in the way of nibbles.

Do the husks eat, drink and sleep? Do husks eat rusks? Maybe we should ask Sheila Ruskin. Ruskin knows everything about husks, rusks and a gentleman's musk. Our own musk is fruity but with savoury notes.

Big Rod Nimrod

One thing that occurs to us about Nimrod is that he must have an awful lot of time on his hands when not busy with his butlering duties. Gabriel Chase can't be the busiest of houses to work in so it makes us wonder what he must do for the rest of the time when he isn't waiting on Josiah Smith hand and foot. Taken out of his own time, Nimrod has found himself in 1883 and has undergone successful training in order to become a manservant, but this job simply can't occupy all of his time. What does he get up to during his time off? Does the role come with a holiday entitlement? He can't spend all day sat in his room picking his arse. Perhaps he has a hobby, or maybe he even has a second job to supplement his earnings that takes him away from the house? What sort of work could a man in his position do? His interests aren't really gone into on screen but we do know that he likes teeth, so the logical extension of this would be that he could work as a dentist or, more likely, a dental nurse. We doubt that Nimrod would have quite the learning to be able to become a dentist, but he'd make a fine nurse and be very good at assisting. He also looks quite natty in a uniform as we can see from his butler outfit, and so would comfortably fit into a nurses' tabard. Back in 1883 dentistry skills were not all that advanced and so the tasks allocated to him by his boss wouldn't be too onerous. We know that Nimrod has evolved from normal Neanderthal status so has a greater intellect than that of his fellows and he would most likely be able to carry out all of the duties required of him in this position.

It would have been interesting if the viewer could've seen Nimrod undergoing his elementary butler training though. He would have had a lot to learn and we suspect that and awful lot of soup was spilled over the training dummies. We bet that he got the cutlery in the wrong order too.

Also, where does Nimrod get his hair done?

Mmm… spilling our soup over training dummies…

Other things that the Doctor hates as well as bus stations and burnt toast but that he forgot to mention to Ace

> Piles
> Davros
> Tetra-Paks / Tetrap axes
> Luton Town FC
> Train spotters
> Timey wimey shit
> His cock being 'cheese-gratered'
> The smell of K9's lubricant
> The word 'squee'
> Acid jazz
> Timmy Mallett

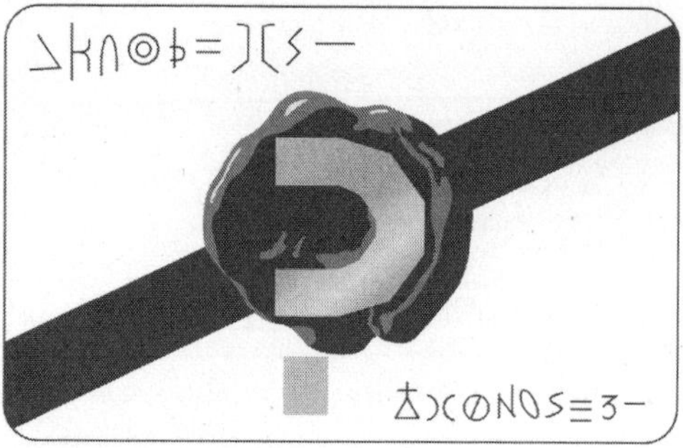

26c – *The Curse of Fenric*

'Make me look like Lana Turner!'

During the second world war, a team of Russian soldiers are sent to capture an encryption machine. They, it and even the chessboards are all cursed. By Fenric.

Jean (or is it Phyllis? I don't know) being sexy. Mmmmm.

A New Leaf

What is that book The Doctor is carrying in his pocket in episode one? It looks pretty big, at least royal format (approximately A5 or Auton-sized for the dense) and has the colour scheme of an A-Z.

Since it doesn't seem to appear as part of the plot itself, we can only theorise as to its importance. And you've probably gathered by now that this is exactly what we're going to do.

There is a clue within *The Curse of Fenric* which you probably missed because you're not as great as us, but we saw it because we're just the best ever at everything as you will know by now because if you read this far there must be a reason. Or you're Ian Briggs and you want to know what we said about your story. Hi, Ian. Anyway – the clue comes quite late in the plot when the Doctor says to Ace 'I need to have a word with your two young friends.'

Why? Why does he need to talk to Jean and Phyllis? He's only briefly ever seen them. There's nothing they could know about that would be of any use to him.

But the book's a clue. That book is clearly a guide for sex tourism in the Whitby area. It's quite big and as we all know, everyone in Whitby is a prostitute.

The Doctor throughout time has proven he has a thing for young girls. He can't keep his hands off them. He's abducted so many over the years.

Jean and Phyllis aren't 'Maidens' as we know from their own admission, and Miss Hardaker knows all too well what girls who go to Maiden's Point have in mind. As does the Doctor. The dirty sod.

'Lak thee woolfs off weentah'

Secret phrases, code words, handshakes and signals are always such cumbersome beasts. The briefing, no doubt on the beach and probably in English, from now on EVERYTHEENK IN EENGLISH, between Sorin and his men must've involved some very last minute decisions on what sort of code word to use in case one of them was in trouble and had to warn the others.

Let's consider this situation for a moment. Sorin has his hands up, held at gunpoint by Millington who knows there are more of Sorin's men nearby. Asked to tell them to give themselves up, Sorin says: 'Lak thee woolfs off weentah!' at which point the guy that looks a bit like The Destroyer without a blue face and horns says 'That's the code word, go, go!' and they leg it.

Millington meanwhile cocks a raised eyebrow, well aware that what's just been said is a very odd thing to say. So why say it? If your code word or phrase is so bloody odd that even a barking mad pot-obsessed loony in the rain can tell it's a secret phrase, why not just yell: 'Run! Go away! Get out of here. It's a trap!'?

Surely if you wanted to keep it quiet, you'd say to your men 'If I say: 'I order you to' before an instruction, then that means run like buggery'. We admit, we're not military men and this probably breaks some sort of protocol, but wouldn't that make more sense than fixing your opponent with a steely gaze and singing 'Lak thee woolfs off weentah!'?

What were their rejected ideas? 'Cam in peas-fully wiv your ands up, lak mice made of treacle in a factory of feathers'? Or 'Cam in peas-fully wiv your ands up, lak sneezes in a vacuum'?

Idiots.

We Play the Contest Again, Time Lord

Fenric, through Judson, announces to the Doctor that they are to 'play the contest again'. As a game whatever they do isn't really up to much (we think that it is something to do with chess and it is just *boorrrriinng* – we could never get on with that **Play Chess** series that the BBC used to put on in the morning during school holidays). It must have taken the Doctor ages to carve the chess pieces for their game out of those bones. Wouldn't it have been better and more interesting if they had decided to settle their differences over something a little more fun? Despite the seriousness of the situation, playing something more interesting than chess would have introduced a degree of levity and entertainment to proceedings. Here are some of the games that they could have played (and remember, just because this story is set during the Second World War, there is no reason that they couldn't have played any of these because the Doctor could have had them all in the TARDIS):

> Conkers
> Ker-Plunk!
> British Bulldog
> Pong
> Noughts and Crosses
> Operation
> Darts
> Cross Fire
> Horace Goes Skiing
> Crossbows and Catapults

Rear Admiral

The seventh Doctor's era is splendid with ranks. Chief Caretakers, Sergeants, Captains, Group Captains, Privates, Knight Commanders, multiple Brigadiers, Intergalactic Captains, Emperors… even old man Burton is a camp commander.

The most baffling of all of these is Captain Sorin. Here is a man who has the respect of his men, is apparently a capable officer and knows which end of his rifle goes bang. Why then does he have such a low opinion of himself?

When asked by Fenric why he was chosen for his mission the only qualification he can think of is that his nan was English. Does this mean the Russians would've gladly sent a postman or a flower arranger to steal the Ultima Machine provided their father or mother's mother was born in England? Does this make any sense to anyone? Even Fenric poo-poos it.

Sorin also ponders that perhaps his ability to speak English got him the mission. While it doesn't seem necessary to do so given that they're meant to sneak in and sneak out with a computer the size of Erato's bog roll in a little tiny dinghy, this does mean he's equally qualified as the rest of his men since for some reason known only to the Russians, from the moment they land ashore they must say everything in English. Why? At no point does this mission involve conversation or 'blending in'. If it did they wouldn't be wearing their Russian uniform.

Is it possible that Sorin's orders got muddled with someone else's? Somewhere there's a translator called Sorin leading an execution squad or driving a tank? Something just isn't right here. But then this Sorin does appear to be linked with Fenric's spooky curse so we definitely have the right guy.
Personally, we think he was sent on a suicide mission because he's crap and no one liked his stupid scarf.

Millington's Marketplace Massacre

In his attempt to get inside the Nazi mind and think how they think, Commander Millington has decked out his office as a replica of the German naval cypher room in Berlin. He's made a good job of it, but it begs the question of just where he has obtained all of this stuff? As there is a war going on, we don't think that as a member of His Majesty's Armed Forces he would realistically be able to travel to Germany to try to get hold of some of this authentic gear, and even if he had been able to then we don't think that the Germans would really have allowed him to buy any of it.

So, was the material being smuggled out of the Reich by somebody specifically for the purpose of creating this ersatz office? We know that during World War II there was an outfit called Special Operations Executive whose job it was to carry out dangerous missions behind enemy lines. Their usual work was mainly concerned with sabotage, assassination and making contact with resistance groups and it is unlikely that Winston Churchill would have given his authority to have them go on a jaunt[1] to redecorate somebody's office no matter how vital Millington considered the plan to be.

An alternative theory is that somebody could be making the items for Millington, but to do this they would need either an original to copy from, or photographs of the original items. Again, this makes us wonder how they got the photographs. They could certainly have been working from old pre-war images, but what if the Berlin office had changed in the meantime and new items had been put in it? We are told that Millington's is an *exact* replica of the original. Could a German double-agent have been providing the crucial information relating to how the cypher office was laid out at a precise

---

[1] **Jaunt** – now available from www.miwk.com

moment in time? This would have been a very risky tactic for any such spy, and we doubt that it would have been really worth the bother for them. If they had been found out by Hitler then they would have been in a very great deal of trouble indeed.

Why is important military funding being spent on accurately mapping that one room when it would be far better spent on mapping the enemy defensive positions?

We're not certain there were any Nazi memorabilia shops in the UK during the war (at least, there was nothing about them in our GCSE History course), and even if there were, then none of the items would even be war mementos at the time. The market for Third Reich collectibles only really came about in the years following the war.

It all seems a little too much trouble to have gone to. We doubt that Hitler, Himmler, Heydrich or Hess had their little offices decked out like Clement Atlee's bathroom or in the same style as the under stairs cupboard of Sir Stafford Cripps.

Where the Hell?

We are told that the story is set at Maiden's Point on the Northumbrian coast. In reality there isn't a Maiden's Point on the Northumbrian coast and the areas that we see in the tale look nothing like Northumbria. Additionally, there weren't any naval bases in the area during World War II (although this is a SECRET naval base, so there might have been). Given the Viking connotations with the story it is a very sensible idea to set the story in such a location but you would have thought that some attempt at getting the locations a little more authentic than they did. Even **Blake's 7** managed to get to Northumbria to film some stories and they weren't even set in the county.

Where the setting very definitely isn't is Whitby as some have suggested. There is no sign of the Abbey or the Magpie Café for a start. The vampiric nature of the hæmovores would have made Whitby a logical setting we suppose but tourists would probably have got in the way of the filming.

No, we think that the story is actually set in and around Lulworth Cove in Dorset and that the Northumbria part of it is all a massive deception.

Let's Find Some Oars

Those Russian soldiers must have biceps like ox legs – there's not a sight of a landing craft anywhere. Surely they didn't paddle all the way over from the mainland? Although, when they do arrive on land and one frightened soldier questions the whereabouts of his comrades, perhaps he's referring to the stinking great ship that should be visible out there on the horizon.

Besides, it's meant to be a super-secret navy base, not just your common or garden encampment – their surveillance systems would be state of the art for the time, so a sneaky submarine or offshore anchor would surely be out of the question. Sonar was first used in 1915, so you'd expect a naval installation to have some of that knocking about at the very least.

(The whole 'houseguests' thing belies the previous paragraph, but surely the soldier on lookout would be a little more surprised that there was just two invaders strolling about, let alone one of them being a girl. After all, invasion forces usually go in a little more mob-handed than that).

Hats off, then, to the plucky Ruskies.

Then again, one of them doesn't appear to be pulling his weight – there are just three paddles in action from the first boat in the underwater shot but up top you can see four of them at it. Presumably one is just going through the motions. Although with that in mind, it's a wonder they make it to the coast at all; they should by rights be going in circles.

'Thecurity, thecurity, thecurity…'

The soldier who follows the Doctor into Judson's office takes his sweet time about it. The Doctor has made introductions, signed a letter and they've all had a jolly chat about logic puzzles before the marine even makes it to the door. The Royal Marine's motto is 'Per Mare, Per Terram' (By Land, By Sea). In a bizarre coincidence, the Latin for 'By Land, By Sea, Very Slowly' is 'Per Mare, Per Terram, Tardissime'.

'Tardis', by the way, is the Latin word for 'Slow' which is rather sweet when you think about it.

But we digress. The point is, for a top secret naval establishment they seem pretty bloody relaxed about breaches of security. Good job the Ruskies didn't get there first as it would have ended up an even shorter story than the Eighth Doctor's swansong.

And it's not just security they're relaxed about. Ace and the Doctor are assigned to joint quarters. Living over the brush, as it were, was as serious a moral offence as mooning His Majesty back in those days. No wonder all those WRENs are so chirpy. It must be like a less crap version of **Carry On England**[2] in the barracks when the lights go out.

---

[2] **Carry On Confidential** – now available from www.miwk.com

Location, Location, Location

By this point, one has to wonder just why people are living in this particular village. Reverend Wainwright, Miss Hardaker, the Doctor and just about everyone they come across talks about there being some kind of evil knocking about. Anyone in their right mind would have scarpered to Bognor years ago, but this lot sit around talking about evil in the most sinister tones possible, while knitting a nice pullover or sipping at the communion wine. The Viking curse runs deep around Maiden's Point, but so, it appears, does a lack of basic comprehension. Evil is bad, therefore getting far away from evil is probably a good idea. Perhaps it's some kind of demonic negative equity that keeps them all fixed firmly in place – even by normal estate agent standards, getting anyone to *want* to move there is going to be a tough sell. The beach looks rubbish; there are sex-starved sailors all over the place, Shouty Judson and, actually come to think of it seemingly nobody else about. Maybe everyone else has scarpered and the reason Hardaker is so bitter is she can't find anyone to buy her cottage so that she can go and move in with her sister Maud in Llandudno.

But then if the Rezzies are happy to live so close to all those 'pain of death' signs, what do we know?

Ace's Faces

Ace's sulky response to Jean and Phyllis when they go for a swim is ever-so-subtly underlined by her pointing at the stonking great sign which reads 'Dangerous Undercurrents'. The sign they're already looking at. Ace is a blunt instrument physically but there are times when we have to ask ourselves whether there's anything much going on upstairs beyond the odd bit of teenage angst and mawkish attempts to lure soldiers into bed. One's teenage years are full of discovery, of awkwardness and uncertainty. It seems that Ace's character has a minimal number of settings. There's violent Ace, sulky Ace, 'Ace!' Ace and Emo Ace. She's not so much an emotional cripple as a textbook teenager with most of the pages missing.

But even by Ace's standards she goes too far when introduced to baby Audrey. Now, we've all met beautiful little girls and boys with the misfortune to have objectionable names. Let's be honest, there are parents out there who put as much thought into the name their poor offspring will have to bear for their whole life as they do into whether it'll be crinkle cut chips tonight or potato waffles for tea. We'll name no names in ridicule, but let's face it - it's going to be hilarious when today's younger generation of Emmas, Samuels, Amelias and Miles are visiting their grandparents in 50 years' time and every octogenarian is named Shaniqua or Kylie or Zak. People name their kids stupidly sometimes.

But not Audrey, Audrey is a perfectly decent name for a youngster in the 1940s and whether Ace has an issue with her mum or not; it's just plain insulting to throw the baby at its mother with as much revulsion as if it had vomited blood out of its face simply because she has a problem with its name. Mrs Dudman shows tremendous restraint in asking in a concerned way if Ace doesn't like it. It's plain to see that Ace would rather be holding a cow pat at this point and if anyone reacted like that to our childrens' names we can likely all agree we'd be rather less lenient. But then, Ace is always turned up to 11 and simply has no emotional response for being confronted with something as cute as a button but is named after someone she hates. It would be slightly more understandable if baby Dudman was named Hitler Bumface Dudman, of course.

But she's not. Bad Ace.

Not just bad, but staggeringly dim Ace, too. Does she really think that the commander of an ultra-secret naval base would actually get away with having an office that's an exact replica of the Nazi's cipher room if there was even the merest hint that he was a German spy? People are in and out of there all day; and as we've seen by this point, he doesn't have a button hidden under his desk that whisks all evidence of his nefarious activities undercover every time somebody knocks on the door. Of course he's not a spy, you dullard. The fact that Ace even has to ask is perhaps the clearest example yet that she's more than just a blunt instrument; she's intellectually blunted beyond redemption.

Moments later, she's asking why everyone around Maiden's Point is so interested in Vikings. It's an infuriatingly dim question given that she's been in the room every time the Doctor unravels another layer of the story that Maiden's Point is built on an old Viking burial ground. The Doctor's reply of 'yes' is ambivalent in the extreme and it's fair to assume that he might be contemplating battering her over her stupid head with that umbrella.

So why, we ask ourselves, does the Doctor keep her around? She's aggressive, violent, over-enthusiastic or clinically miserable from one moment to the next. The Doctor, by this point has developed a more questionable choice of companion than he's had in the past. Mel, let's face it, was enthusiastic to the point where you sometimes just wanted to slap her and tell her to have a chamomile tea and calm the fuck down, but at least she knew how to use a computer and scream about the place convincingly.

The Doctor's choice of Ace as a travelling companion seems to be largely driven by his desire not to get his hands dirty but to still be able to cause a bit of havoc every now and then. And possibly to help Ace get the fuck over herself. But why he'd want to do that is beyond us. She's easy on the eye but the very definition of high maintenance and more often than not everything she touches is soon in dire need of some maintenance too. The seventh Doctor is most certainly a dark and mysterious character, but there are times when he's a bit of an idiot. No wonder he's covered in question marks. That's not the design of the jumper, those are just nature's astounded puzzlements made ethereal.

Let's pick another example to illustrate that theory – he and Ace stomp along the shingle beach whereupon they discover a dead Russian soldier. Superb observational powers which are immediately outweighed by the fact that seven more manage to sneak up on them completely unnoticed.

Notice, by the way, that when Ace demands of the Doctor 'Am I so stupid?' his reply is somewhat less than qualified… 'No, that's not it'. Our case is rested.

But against all evidence of her imbecility, Ace is the one who finally cracks the code and identifies the Viking inscriptions as a logic diagram. It turns out she's right, but we're certain that's guesswork, prompted by the fact that she was playing with the flip flop puzzle moments before. If you see a picture of a beautiful, naked man/woman/manwoman the first thought to enter your head is 'phwoar! I would.' Well, it's basically that. Ace has no clue what the logic diagram is but the very act of playing with the toy causes her to assume the next things she sees is also a logic puzzle. Good job, then, that she wasn't on her way to the loo or playing Operation.

Although it must be said that Judson jumps on the theory rather too eagerly. As a scientist, you'd hope he'd require just the tiniest bit of evidence.

It's an Old Wall… It Waits

Just what is it that makes the missing Viking inscriptions in the crypt flare into existence? The impression is very much that Millington's reading of the translation is some kind of incantation. That would certainly play to the idea that Fenric has been playing the long game. It takes a brilliant mind and a heck of a lot of patience to lay a trap like that, bearing in mind that it is the words being read aloud in English that sets things moving. But what about the Reverend's grandfather? He originally translated the inscriptions, oh, a hundred years-or-so before. When he did so, did Fenric rise, only to discover that the Doctor hadn't turned up yet? No wonder he's so crazy when he does finally meet our heroes. Nobody likes to be disturbed from a restful slumber, dreaming of world domination, only to find out it's a doddery old cleric and not an all-powerful Time Lord who's dragged you out of bed. Plus, it must have been a nightmare getting that wall re-rendered. We never learn the fate of Wainright the senior, but presumably his battered corpse is laying somewhere in Fenric's bedroom having been given a thoroughly good kicking. Demi-gods are not known for their forgiveness.

Speaking of playing the long game, Millington's desperation to uncover the Viking code is just a snapshot of the kind of intricate plotting the players in this game have established so that they can all be in that one place at that one time. Now, we know that Millington is probably connected to the family buried in the churchyard and that he and Judson go back a long way. So presumably both are local boys. Immensely driven and determined local boys because they each managed to orchestrate that they would be there, back home where it all started, running a top secret (although by now we think we can all agree that it really isn't) naval installation designed ostensibly to decrypt German U-boat transmissions but in reality to unleash Fenric.

Such forethought and manipulation of two lives, let alone those of everybody else in the camp, village and beyond, is staggering and it's easy to see why the Doctor is so taken aback when he realizes that all the pieces have fallen into place.

Fenric must have been monumentally pissed off at Wainwright's grandfather to go to those sort of lengths.

In fact Millington's attitude in general leaves a lot to be desired. Quote a few words of ancient Norse to the chap and he'll gladly reveal his entire plan. He goes from pointing a gun at the Doctor to inviting him back to his room for a sleepover within moments and all the Doctor has to do is recite a bit of old poetry at him. What does that prove? If we were looking to get balls deep in a mystery and we knew that mystery was somehow linked to ancient Norse, then the first thing we'd do is pop along to the library (the closest thing they had to Google in those days) and bone up (stop sniggering, you pathetic oaf) on a few choice verses to win the locals over. But the Doctor didn't even have to do that – he's got the bloody TARDIS. Another theory about *The Curse of Fenric* that's starting to form is that the tale hinges on rather a lot of gullible people and more than its fair share of coincidences. Is that chess? Because Fenric and the Doctor seem to think so. To us it sounds more like roulette, and Russian roulette at that (see what we did there?).

Quick Nurse, the Screens!

The delectable Nurse Crane – what a fine figure of a woman she is, and with the patience of a saint. All she does all day is push Shouty Judson about and hold his Davey lamp, and what does she get in return? Constant abuse from everyone around her. Dangerous undercurrents indeed – there has to be more to their relationship than that and perhaps it's just the sight of a nurse's uniform and a stern gaze, but it's tempting to think there's a little more to their relationship than meets the eye. We don't know the extent of Judson's injuries, but she seems quite happy manhandling him. Let's return to the odd couple later while we all have a collective ponder on that one.

The Best Laid Plans

When Millington's plans for the Ultra Machine are finally revealed, can you spot the flaw? The Ultima Machine is the most sophisticated computing device on the planet and the Ruskies want to steal its 'brain'. All well and good – because the Tommies are all up for that if it means they can secrete some of the poison that lives under Maiden's Point into the device so that it wipes out the Russians when they get home. It's a cunning and arguably quite evil plan, but given the times it's most assuredly plausible. Except they don't secrete anything – they attach an enormous glass vial full of Day-Glo green goo to the Ultima's brain with a few wires and an angle bracket. And they really think the Russian's won't notice. With thinking like that from the War Office it's a miracle we weren't wiped out the day Mr Chamberlain waved the piece of paper that Hitler had just wiped his arse on.

1. It's a machine and in those days computing devices were powered by gears, cogs and, you know, MACHINERY. There was no such thing as organic computing in the 1940s, a technology we're only just beginning to unravel here in the 21st Century. Let's hope the boffins working on that one have seen **Sapphire & Steel** or we could all be in trouble. But the point is there is no way anyone is going to be suckered into believing that a glass jar filled with green liquid is an actual part of the Ultima device.

2. The liquid glows very brightly and very greenly, which makes hiding it extremely tricky.

3. They don't try to hide it. Millington tells the Doctor to look deep into the machine but in all honesty you can see it right there behind the rotary coggy buttony thing that Judson keeps tinkering with. It couldn't be more obvious if they'd stuck a dirty great sign on the device with an arrow saying "Do Not Touch This Poison Until Back in Russia"

It Feels All Tingly

Twilight, **True Blood** and their ilk have a lot to answer for, glamming up vampirism into something dangerous but beautiful and seductive. Indeed, Jean and Phyllis when they first appear in ~~vampire~~ hæmovore form are the definition of vamp, at least visually. Their attempts at sexy talk are terrible, particularly for two girls who earlier confessed to not being 'maidens' (you, know, they've done it and everything) anymore. The Russian soldier on the beach thankfully doesn't speak English fluently, so he's well up for it. They're effectively narrating the scene for the hard of hearing, which is very kind, but aside from each other the only person there is the Russian, and as we've established if he's going to be taken in by those two his English must be terrible.

The effect of Fenric on its victims is to be questioned. Jean and Phyllis betray (albeit unconvincingly) their tarty roots after they are first converted by luring the idiot soldier to his death. But to then go straight after Miss Hardaker suggests they retain some of their human memories and are therefore every bit the slutty, nasty little bitches that Hardaker first made them out to be. All Fenric seems to have done is amplify their slutty nastiness and make their fingernails grow out.

We're left wondering whether their toenails are similarly affected – being taken over by Fenric seems to have some kind of effect on keratin in general because the girls also adopt proper big 80s hairdos the minute they're turned into ~~vampires~~ hæmovores. Given that possession apparently also renders them unable to walk at anything faster than a moonwalk-like gait (akin to an astronaut, not like Michael Jackson, although, to be fair the latter would be amazing) it's highly likely that their toenails have indeed grown to a similar degree as their fingernails and, trapped within their footwear, are making walking normally hellishly difficult even for a ~~vampire~~ hæmovore. Could this perhaps be the universal theory as to why monsters generally lumber about the place? Such movement is rarely menacing although the added roar, or in this case the archly-delivered insult, does enhance the effect, but any victim worth their salt could simply run away. The two girl ~~vampires~~ hæmovores clearly think they're achieving Cowerd-like levels of wit with their husky threats but the overall effect, what with the big hair, the nails and the mawkish attempts to appear sexually charged, is really just uncomfortable. And not in a trouser way.

Maybe the likes of us are just built of sterner stuff than your average randy soldier, tired old lady or ecclesiastically challenged vicar.

And so the girls cut a swathe of destruction through the village while the ~~vampires~~ hæmovores emerge from the deep to reclaim their treasure, or whatever it is they're supposed to be doing. It's not really all that clear, other than Being Monsters. Now they have a valid reason for the slow, lumbering gait – they've been decomposing underwater for centuries, so they're bound to be new to all that walking on land business. Which by the same logic, means that the outstretched hands aren't meant to appear menacing at all, they're merely holding them out to steady themselves.

Sorin Through Chests Lak Naaarfs froo Buttah

As the Russian soldiers stand at the cliff top and watch the ~~vampires~~ hæmovores make their inexorable way towards the village, the Captain and one of his men talk about legends of vampires and, says the soldier, that they don't exist. At this point, Captain Sorin pulls one of several wooden stakes out of the backpack of the soldier in front of him and begins sharpening it. Now that really is a monumentally convenient happenstance. Did the Russians bring a ready supply of stakes along only for some of their number to have absolutely no idea why? Even if they gathered the wood from the nearby forest, somebody must surely have questioned why they were carrying around in a backpack?

Later, as Sorin and his men spot Ace being manhandled by the ~~vampires~~ hæmovores atop the church, the very first thing they do is chuck the bag of stakes away and run at the ~~vampires~~ hæmovores with their guns. One clever soldier even remembers to take his bag of wood with him to the rooftop, but still proceeds to shoot at the monsters for a few minutes before driving a stake through them and reducing them to goo.

She's Got the Horn

Ace only clapped eyes on Sorin moments before and already she's making eyes at him and accepting his scarf as a token to remember him by. The slut. She was like this with Mike in *Remembrance of the Daleks*. It's clear Ace likes a man in uniform or at the very least one with rank to pull.

But she's at it again now in her attempts to distract the guard. Look, there's a war on – times are hard and there's bromide in the tea, but were people really so desperate for a bit of nookie?

That rubbish that she comes out with in order to lure the soldier away from his post goes beyond mawkishness into a whole new realm of, well, we're not quite sure what it is. But rest assured, if a girl tried that kind of bollocks on with any of us when we offered to buy her a drink, we'd move along sharpish and tell the barman that she's probably had enough already. Sorin seems pretty taken in by her silly sexuality too, so maybe times really were that hard.

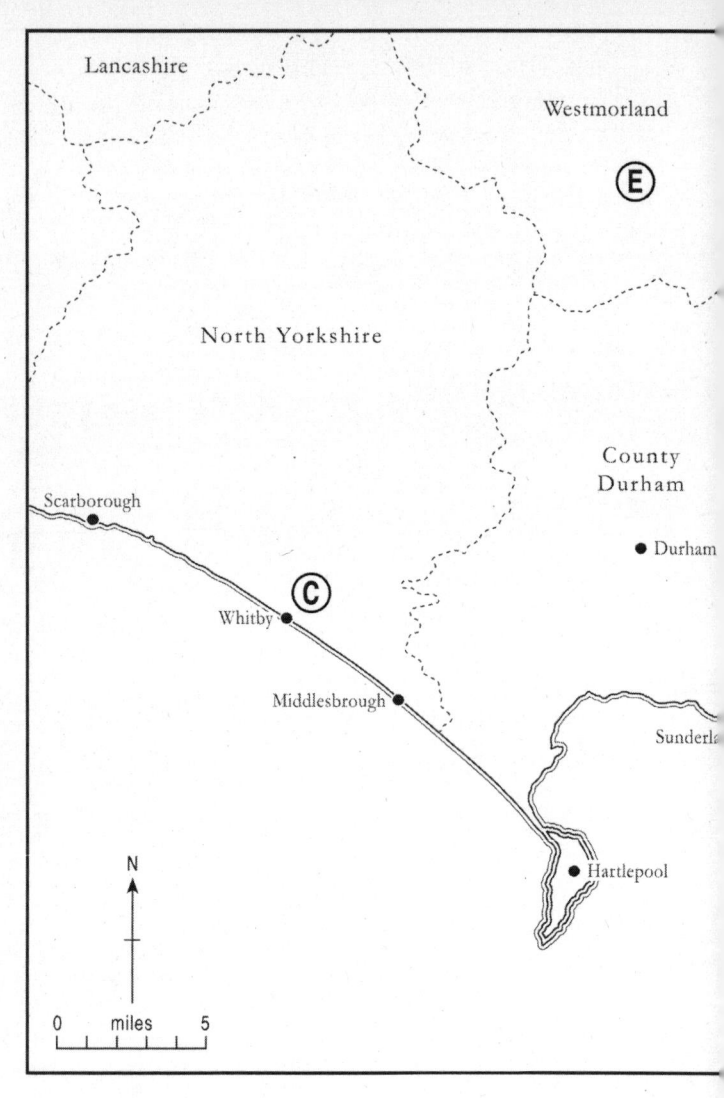

Map of North-east England used by invading Soviet soldiers, later captured by British Intelligence

© *Crown Copyright HMSO / War Office, 1937*

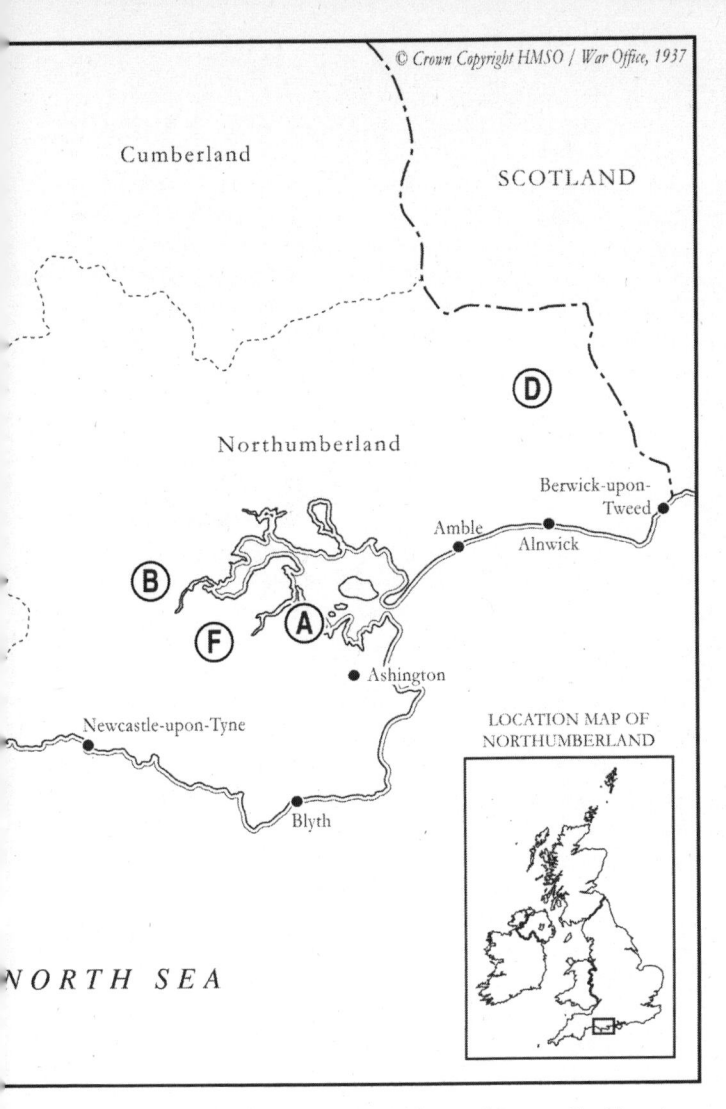

A—Landing point   B—Secret British Naval Base   C—Vampires
D—Faster than the Second Hand on a Watch?   E—Westeros
F—St. Jude's Church

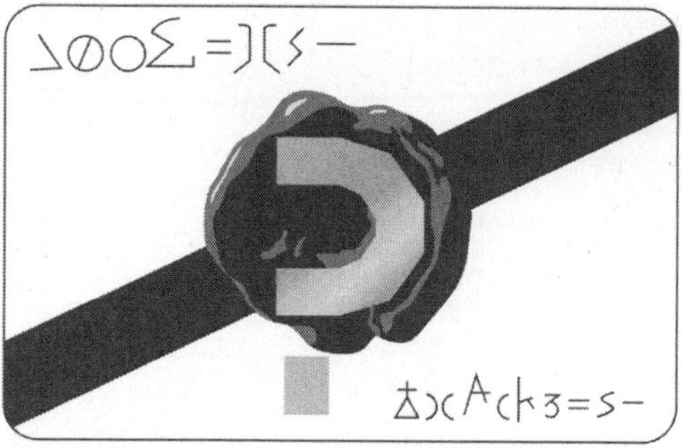

26d – *Survival*

> *'Can't. Hayfever.'*

The Doctor is lured by the Master to the planet of the Cheetah People which is slowly being destroyed.

The Master, pretty proud of the Cheetah People pants he has just finished perfecting.

Dave's Mum

In Perivale, Dave's mum is the stuff of legend. Her meals, particularly her dinners, are the talk of the town. If you're peckish and it's somewhere between dawn and dusk, why not nip to Dave's house because his mum will always be cooking dinner.

Sunday morning. It's Sunday morning. The Doctor and Ace arrive in Perivale on Sunday morning. So why then is Dave's mum putting his dinner on the table? Is it still there from last night and she's been waiting for an opportunity to tell him? Dave's not only up bright and early to wash his car, when most people would be lighting a fire on Horsenden Hill, but he's also been rolling around in the road with his wet sponge just moments before being stalked by a massive cat on a horse. We can tell because there's a wet patch and a bit of foam right behind him.

But look, dinner is geographically a midday or evening meal. It's definitely never used to describe breakfast, except apparently by Dave's mad mum. More to the point, even if it is freshly cooked why the hell is she cooking him dinner? He's in the middle of washing his car! There's been a major scheduling catastrophe here and either Dave's mum is cooking him dinner while he washes the car to annoy him, or Dave's washing the car to avoid her dinner.

This throws our opening statement out of whack. Perhaps she's the most appalling cook, but prolific in the kitchen leading the people of Perivale to do whatever they can to avoid her bloody dinners?

What did she make for Dave's dinner anyway? Whatever it was, we know it's small enough to be placed on a table so that rules out a full spit-roasted pig or horse. It's Sunday so a roast would make sense.

But we can't get over this exchange:

> 'Dave, your dinner's on the table!'
>
> 'Alright, Mum.'

Oh Dave, poor Dave. Such a terribly sad life he has. Let's see what we can infer from his brief appearance.

Dave is a man in his early thirties who still lives with his mum. Now, the interesting thing about Dave's relationship with his mother is that she calls him Dave, not David. Assuming that Mrs Mum is not suffering from the rare disease Triggeritis, a form of mild Tourettes which causes everyone to be referred to as 'Dave', this is suggestive of a worrying distance in the relationship between mother and son. Not to this family is the son always referred to by his full title of David; rather Mother attempts to awkwardly connect with her son by using the shortened version of his name, Dave, just as his mates would use if he had any. The two have never been particularly close, yet Dave continually has to attend to her needs in their own private behind-closed-doors world. Dave was either never breast-fed as a child or was breast-fed up until the age of 8, and this has had a lasting impact on his relationship with his ailing mother. We're getting hints and subtexts here of Timothy Lumsden in **Sorry!**

Dave wears jeans while washing the car, a concession to the cool and trendy characters he's seen on television, stomping around the **EastEnders** or **The Bill** versions of London with their modern denim trousers on display for all to see. However, he gets it badly wrong. Dave tucks his tragically unfashionable navy, green and white hoopy polo-shirt into his jeans, in the style of a middle-aged, middle-class, middle-of-the-road father desperate to appear tidy in front of the curtain-twitching neighbours. As soon as Dave gets indoors with his Mum for his tea, the jeans come off, the watch disappears from his wrist, and Dave is straight into his pyjamas and bed-socks as his Mum spoon-feeds him chicken soup while they watch **The Antiques Roadshow**.

Dave's losing his hair, a result of male-pattern baldness probably inherited from his mother's paternal line: just another reason that Dave severely resents his mother and talks to her in such a condescending fashion. The baldness prevents him from coming off quite as he'd intended and he gets no interest from attractive passers-by, not even the long-haired guitarist with the leather jacket and motorcycle at Number 42.

Dave may be washing his car but he's clearly never been allowed to drive it: his mother would turn blue at the very thought. Dave couldn't be trusted to handle a car on his own. Dave always wanted a car but his parents would not let him have one and he fulfils his fantasies of car-ownership by going through the routine of washing this car every Sunday: first a heavy working over with the sponge, then a light rinsing down with the hose and bucket, and finally a lengthy waxing process using the latest product bought from Halfords and a deep buffing into the nooks and crannies with a *faux*-leather chamois. Despite his love of the large blue automobile, Dave actually rides about town on a red and yellow BMX bike with no gears, those plastic bread-bag fasteners on the brake cables, and a playing card in the spokes to mimic the sound of a motor going FFFRRRSHH when the wheels turn. Sometimes, when his Mum isn't looking, he doesn't wear his yellow helmet and shin-guards.

The car in question is a dreary blue saloon car, apparently a Vauxhall Cavalier Mk2. This was the UK's second-most popular model of car in 1984 and 1985, showing both Dave's family's complete lack of imagination when purchasing exciting automobiles and their constant behind-the-times mentality. Whose then is the car? Well, it's clear from the absence of a father figure in the sequence that Mr Dad died years ago, probably of a broken heart as a result of the way his son turned out. Dave maintains the car in pristine condition as a shrine to his father's memory, and ritually finishes it off by hand (don't titter) every weekend as a way of, in his own mind, connecting with his long-lost father in a way that he never managed to do while he was alive. Suspicious about the whole situation, we checked the car's registration plate (B765 VYL) with the DVLA, and the number is in fact registered to a red Jaguar XJS. The use of a patently false number-plate raises serious questions about the nature of Mr Dad's business dealings, throwing doubt on the integrity of his character and suggesting that perhaps Dave's idolisation of his father may have been based on an entirely unsound premise.

At the end of the sequence, Dave's circle is complete: tired of life yet with little to no hope for the future, this timid, diffident wretch's life ends in the only way it could have done. Forever the victim, Dave is transported to an alien world with a pink sky by a cat on horseback and in short order is eaten by starving felines: the very pets typically associated with a middle-class urban household led by a domineering, ageing mother. In what can only be described as an irony of the most extreme of proportions, Dave's background has killed him.

Such is Dave's luck with the rest of humanity and the sadness of his life that he isn't even given a credit at the end of Part One. We did a bit of research into Dave (as you can tell) and can reveal two surprising facts: he's actually one of the Wolves of

Fenric, and is physically identical to one of the Russian Soldiers in *The Curse of Fenric* (clearly a grandfather). The paucity of his situation is so moving that it was remembered twenty-one years later when Dave appeared again, in full clown make-up, in a hotel room in 2010's *The God Complex*. A lesson to us all.

Ace Flees

We're sure Ace was probably a fairly sensible, practical girl at a point prior to *Dragonfire* and her meeting the Doctor. But something about his 'end of episode' suicide attempt on a sheer cliff-face has clearly rubbed off on her.

In *Remembrance of the Daleks* she has two opportunities to walk across a classroom. Remember when you were at school, especially in the science labs, and the only way to get from one end to the other was *over* the desks rather than around them? Ace has clearly developed an ability to be incredibly impractical about her escapes.

Example one: 'Who are you calling small?'
Ace is standing next to a Dalek by the double door entrance to the classroom. The Dalek is through the door, Ace is behind the door (which opens both ways). She could, if she wanted, sneak out behind it and run back down the stairs. Instead she shouts (from behind it) and then proceeds to smash the Kaled shit out of it with a baseball bat consequently blinding it. She is now *next to* a blind Dalek, by a set of open doors that the Dalek isn't actually blocking. In her breakneck assessment of the situation she immediately sees the route of escape. As the Dalek hits a literal 'blind panic' she runs in front of it (the end that shoots people and is currently shooting the shit out of the opposite end of the classroom, shots which somehow manage to miss a whole

wall of windows as we'll see later) she then runs across the back of the classroom, still under fire, hops up onto a desk, kicks all the shit out of the way (who puts all that shit back for later on?) and leaps through a window which, given the age of the school, is presumably a metal frame. She then runs downstairs (better plan, it takes them several minutes to negotiate a flight of these) into an outside area with a huge entrance (the one the Doctor and ~~UNIT~~ Counter Measures use in the next episode) but rather than running out that way she runs to the middle of the room and kneels down.

Example two: 'Ace, get away from that window!'
Ace is standing by the window. She needs to get from the window to where the Doctor, Alison, Gilmore and Rachel are standing. She has moved to the window in a few seconds just previous to this. Rather than retracing her steps, Ace instead climbs onto the desk, kicks all the shit off the desk (after someone, probably Rachel, tidied it all up from earlier) and hops off to join the others crouching behind the desk. Several seconds later, the windows are blown in. She could've squatted on the ground and slid over on her arse quicker and more safely.

Example three: 'Gordon Bennett!'
This one is partly the Doctor's fault. The go-cart in *The Happiness Patrol* is hardly an ideal getaway vehicle.

Example four: 'Ehhh, iz too-againz wun, owzabout the cock sick muff?'
Ace identifies the perfect escape from the church in *The Curse of Fenric* is not the back door, but up the stairs to the top of a tower and then descending said tower on a rope ladder directly into the pile of ~~vampires~~ hæmovores they were attempting to beat off (stop it!) in the first place.

Example five: 'Girl, you need pussy control.'

We're up to present day and Ace is sitting on a playground swing, stroking her pussy. Behind her a fucking great cat in a waistcoat sitting on a horse materialises and roars at her. Quick-thinking Ace immediately drops the cat and runs to… the slide! This is the *Fenric* escape all over again. Up and over and back into danger. The slide has no advantages whatsoever. There is nothing, save for the merest hint of a chance that this particular Cheetah Person likes slides, that suggests she's any safer standing on top of the slide than she would be smearing her face in Whiskas and screaming 'Lick my tuna face!'. She continues to try out all the playground's attractions before finally installing herself inside a large metal cage. This is, in all fairness to Ace, the safest place she could go. It's around this point that she screams for the Doctor. Having noticed that the Cheetah Person can't get his/her horse through the gaps of the climbing frame Ace immediately plunges herself into danger by leaving the Cage of Playground Safety and legging it across a field. This being, to her mind, her best chance at greater safety since we all know humans can outrun horses. Stupid, stupid girl.

In for a Penny…

If the McCoy/Cartmel era has shown us anything, it's that 'money makes the world go round'. Previously in **Doctor Who** money was barely worthy of a mention. Pitch and toss and skanking Lanzarotean (what do they call themselves?) waiters aside, the Doctor rarely had a need to shake his coin sack in the face of anyone.

Within just three seasons money is rife. In *Paradise Towers* the Doctor smashes up a public phone and swipes the cash. Lovely little Tucker-esque coins which not only come to the same value as a phone call in Paradise Towers, but also one of them is worth a whole can of Fizzade. Very refreshing.

It doesn't end though, *Delta and the Bannermen* opens with a toll fee, the Doctor has a price on his head because the guy from the *Flying Pickets* only kills for enjoyment, even though he also does it for money. When we say 'does it for money' we can't prove that. But he does kill for money. Not the bloke from the *Pickets* but the character he's playing who looks like the bloke from the *Pickets* who doesn't prostitute himself. Except for the BBC in the late eighties.

Glitz sells his crew, Kane can't stop giving young girls (preferably with fire in their bellies) shiny coins and his whole villainous empire is a shop. Then in *Remembrance of the Daleks* the Doctor gives Ace some cash for breakfast (let's not go into that again), she counts out coins on the table and Mike goes to great lengths to explain the local currency. Shortly after on Terra Alpha we have a Waiting Zone with a fruit machine which takes coins, and both the Doctor and the Kandy Man use a coin, one to decide which person who actually accused him of being a Pimplehead he'll kill first, the other to illustrate just how shitty life actually is.

Ace steals some gold coins paid to the mathematician by Lady Peinforte and uses them to dispatch billions of rather weak aurumphobic Cybermen. In *Greatest Show in the Galaxy* … well we'll leave that one for now, but in *Battlefield* the Doctor turns out his pockets with a number of unusual currencies, Josiah lobs a fat wad of notes at the Doctor in *Ghost Light*, and in *Survival* Ace wins a sodding great pile of cash on yet another fruit machine.

The eighties are supposed to be the decade of greed. If **Doctor Who** was anything to go by, that's some true shit right there.

Flippin' Cats

Have you ever been kept awake at night by cats? If you had, the one thing you'll be all too familiar with is the yell of 'If we fight like animals, we die like animals!' being screamed at top volume.

Science has yet to establish how cats can form these words, or indeed if they know their true meaning in English. But it's an established fact that when you hear these words yelled loudly in the street during the day, it means flippin' cat fights are happening in your flippin' street.

FACT.

Fully Clothed Pussy

The Cheetah People have been derided in the past for looking too much like teddy bears. Quite frankly, if your teddy bear looked like that when you were a kid, odds are you had a psychopath for a parent. The Cheetah People look good and no different to the *identical* Cat People in the new series.

That aside, there are some issues with the Cheetah People – but then you've probably worked out how this book works by now. Very well done, you for sticking with it all this way. If you're reviewing this book, please use the word 'honeypotterific' in the text to prove you read the whole thing.

Anyway, the Cheetah People are a slight mystery. It's not clear if they're related to the Kitlings or not, but they do seem to be humans who are possessed by the unnamed planet. For the sake of argument, we're going to call it Wowzville Beta 14.

Now the Cheetah People are living on a jolly hot planet. One look at it and you know it's hot. If the flaming lakes and red smoke-filled sky aren't clues enough, people do occasionally say things like 'Phew it's hot' or 'Crikey, getting a bit of a sweat on'. It's really hot.

So why then do the Cheetah People, essentially cats and animal by nature, wear clothes? Well here at Auton Towers (shaped like a giant phallus with a garden to match) we've formulated a few theories and observations.

The first and most irksome one, which we'll resolve shortly, is the issue of the Cheetah People wearing those beaded necklaces. Cheetah People are very cat-like and as such have paws. Those paws are big padded things with no opposable digits (although we do see them carrying weapons and holding reins so work that one out!). How then to they made a beaded necklace? More to the point, how do they make any of their clothes or little houses or dance stage (that raised platform outside the Master's tent)?

Obviously they can't. Even if they're borrowing clothes from carrion supplied by the Kitlings, surely that would leave them decked out like an eighties South London chav? All shell suits and piano key ties. This wouldn't be anywhere near as threatening, but we know that cats are quite vain. They preen themselves all day long so it's not impossible.

The favoured likelihood, and indeed the most enjoyable, is that their clothes, necklaces, houses and dance stage were built and crafted by the Master.

By this stage in the game, the Master (in Tremas' smelly old corpse) has become quite the mad man. Mind you, it all starts as early as *Time Flight* where he gladly plays Kalid for no readily apparent reason other than to prat about for his own amusement. We then get the daftness of *Mark of the Rani* where he pretends to be a scarecrow, again for no real reason.

So by now it's quite possible that he thinks biscuits are playing cards and pencils are swords. It's quite hot on Wowzville Beta 14 so couple the sweaty feverishness with his usual delusional state and we have a man who sits giggling in a desert while making necklaces, shirts and dance stages for giant cats.

We even briefly see his practical side as he rapidly fashions a collar and lead for Midge (Just the start, Midge. Just the start…) from the guts of an old dead horse. This is a man who's handy. He probably knocked up that poncey cravat from old fish skin or dried blueberries.

Going back a bit – does this mean the Master can juggle? Those are after all silver juggling balls he uses to distract the Cheetah People. Once he's dressed them in his little outfits is he making them take part in some twisted Wowzville Beta 14 talent show on that little stage? If so can Cheetah People applaud? Maybe that's why the Master's so uptight. All that entertainment and effort and they can't express their appreciation. No applause or cheers just … catcalling. Sorry.

What Would Midge Like for Pudding?

Just the tart, Midge. Just the tart.

Ace's Gang

Ange is quite clearly hopped up on some kind of illegal substance. The slack jaw, the slurred speech and disinterested outlook on life – there's nothing to suggest that Perivale itself is any kind of soul-sucking locale, so that one's clearly up to no good. Ange reckons it's hayfever, but we're having none of that.

If we follow the whole 'survival of the fittest' motif, then presumably those of Ace's mates who we meet on Wowzville Beta 14 are the best that Perivale has to offer. And if Ace can set herself up as their leader so easily then the best that Perivale has to offer really isn't much to write home about. Unless of course you're writing to complain (never give up on a joke). Up to now, they've been treating their experiences as some kind of outward bounds holiday gone wrong.

The gang does acquit itself pretty well when they're trying to rescue the milkman who appears out of nowhere, despite ignoring the Doctor's commands to stay still. He's quite right in that one is supposed to stand perfectly still while a cheetah has its sport, for fear of attracting its attention. But screaming as much at the top of one's voice would have the same effect as running up to it and tickling it under the chin. The point about staying still is all about not appearing obvious lest the cheetah take a sudden interest in you. The Doctor couldn't be more obvious if he tried. He should damn well be grateful to those kids for drawing the cheetah away, if anything. But no, he stands there ranting at them while they do all the hard work. Sometimes, the Doctor is hard to love.

Cats

Bloody hell that cat in Perivale looks scary! Now here at Auton we're well known for our love of cats, but that ugly bugger can stay well away. Not quite sure what its problem is but it's clearly some kind of alien moggy, a giant, shape-changing one too if poor old Dave is anything to go by.

Now, the black cat we see on Earth, we think it is implied, turns into a cheetah the moment it arrives on Wowzville Beta 14. And on Earth, when it kidnaps a human it changes into a cheetah before doing so. So, presumably the whole black cat thing is just to lure unsuspecting victims. Or are the cats some kind of inter-dimensional portal? We hope not, because the thought of where the cheetahs enter and exit the poor thing is not a pleasant one.

But what of the cats on Wowzville Beta 14 who remain as cats? Look, there they are, scavenging at the remains left behind by their big brothers and sisters. Are they pets? Is there a cat caste hierarchy, like in **Planet of the Apes**? Clearly, the moggies are the Wowzville Beta 14 equivalent of chimps… lowly types who carry out the menial task of ingesting and expunging their masters from one planet to the next. The cheetah themselves are probably the gorillas – warlike and driven purely by instinct. We don't see any other types of cat around the place, so presumably the Master is the closest thing they have to Doctor Zaius. No wonder the place is falling to pieces. If **Doctor Who** history has shown us anything it's that anyone who hooks up with the Master is on a fast-track to oblivion.

Meet a Cheetah

No wonder Dave and the other chap are so terrified when the Cheetah People spring out of thin air atop their trusty steeds.

Cos-play wasn't as well-known back in the pre-Internet days, but it was still going on behind the pampas-grassed front lawns of seemingly every day suburban households. Wife swapping, as a kink, we can get our heads around – after all, variety is the spice of life and as long as all parties are in agreement why not indulge in a little bit of naughtiness with the woman from next door. S&M? Sure, if you want a bit of spanking, why not? But Furries? That defies logic. Are those involved doing so because they really want to have sex with the actual animals themselves or is it the fantasy of 'being' the animal that turns them on? Either way, Perivale is awash with funny little people dressed in cat outfits riding about on horses. It's a curious way to spend your Sunday afternoon, but as we say, as long as all concerned are up for it then we can grudgingly allow them on their way. But this lot take the biscuit – without so much as a 'would you stroke this' they're chasing unsuspecting members of the public down the street with god only knows what sexual nastiness in mind. It's sickening behaviour which is doubtless leading to some kind of Furry/horse/rape type scenario.

What's that? They really are cats? On horses? REALLY? Oh… oh, okay.

Well it's still not right, of course, but given that they're creatures from another planet we shouldn't expect anything less. Randy furries on horseback would make for a far more terrifying adventure, though.

But why are the Cheetah People kidnapping kids and transporting them to Wowzville Beta 14? And what happens to them when they get there? The cheetahs who do the transporting don't seem to be anywhere close by when they perform that nasty trick, so is it just for fun? Well, no – as Ace is soon to discover our old friend Dave is sleeping with the pussies. The cheetahs, like all cats, are merely playing with their prey –

lulling them into a false sense of security before appearing in a blaze of light and running them down. Thinking about it, they could have just as easily done that back on Earth, but there's nothing like a bit of razzmatazz if you want to scare your victim out of their wits.

Ace's cat-friend Kara comes to an untimely end at the end of the Master's pointy claw. But there's one more surprise in store – she turns back into a human! So just how many of those on Wowzville Beta 14 are really humans in disguise? Does the planet take all-comers and turn them into cats? If so, who really cares if the planet does blow itself to bits? The cheetahs that are left there just before things go pop disappear into nowhere – presumably heading back home to wherever they came from (Wowzville Beta 15?). So all's well that ends well, really. Apart from the Master – but he gets what he deserves as always.

Harvey & Len

This is the Big Finish spin-off that has yet to happen.

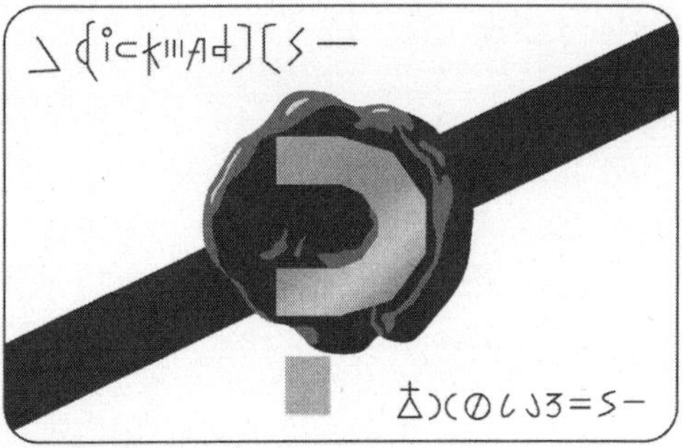

BEYOND THE SCHEDULE

Doctor Who was taken off air after *Survival*. Having had a taster in 1985 of what happens when you cancel a programme with such a rabid following, this time the BBC opted to never actually say it was cancelled. 'I killed it!' said Sylvester McCoy at the 50th Anniversary convention in London. No you didn't, Sylv. You were well on your way to saving it.

Of course, between *Survival* and 2005's *Rose* there were some occasional dalliances on TV. We've concerned ourselves only with those that feature the Seventh Doctor.

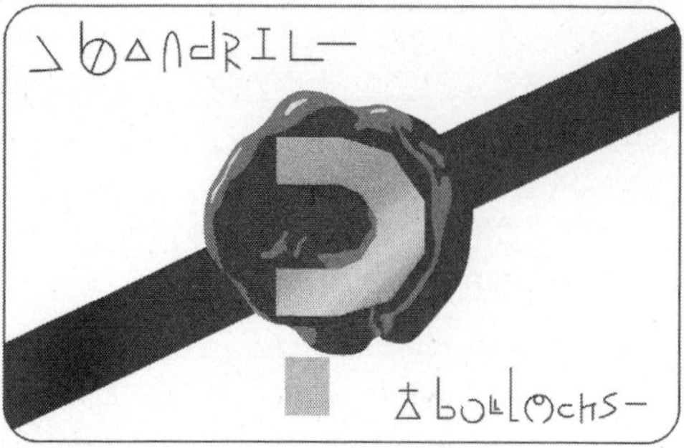

1993 – *Dimensions in Time*

Doctor Who reaches its 30th birthday. Bill Clinton becomes president of the US, The Campaign for Homosexual Law Reform succeeds in having the Irish sodomy law reformed and the World Trade Center is bombed. Nobody remotely interesting to us is born because it would make them too young for us to find tolerable in 2014. We lose Audrey Hepburn, Les Dawson, Vincent Price, Anthony Burgess, Federico Fellini and tragically Stephen Lawrence and James Bulger. The highest grossing US film is **Jurassic Park**.

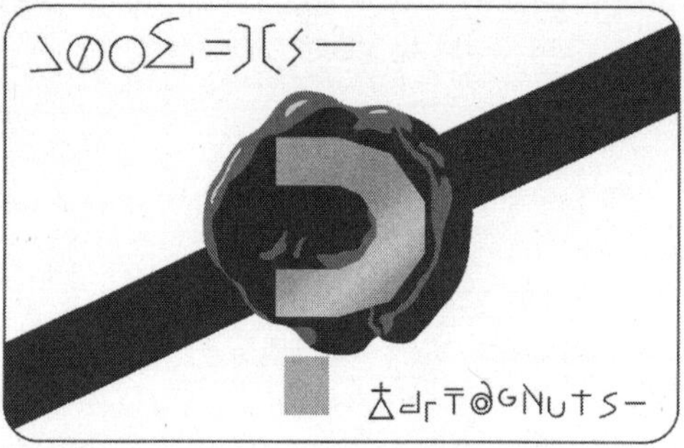

1993 – *Dimensions in Time*

'Pickled in time, like gherkins in a jar'

The Rani is back, this time with a fiendish plan to trap all the surviving and available actors from the BBC TV series **Doctor Who** in the other BBC TV series **EastEnders** together with a bunch of old threadbare costumes and props.

A Cunning Plan

The Rani's plan seems straightforward enough, despite its deli-based analogies. By trapping the Doctors in some kind of bizarre time loop, she hopes to drive them insane. Fair enough and broadly consistent with her antics up to this point. Mind you, she could have saved herself a lot of time and effort by simply locking the TARDIS doors and putting regular old **EastEnders** episodes on an unbreakable stream via the TARDIS monitor. Quite what putting them into Albert Square does above and beyond subjecting them to the miseries and unassailable futility of enduring the lives of the eponymous cockneys by proxy isn't made clear. We know she likes a good old gloat, though, so it's probably just that.

There's also the additional bonus of giving them all neck strain by influencing the chain of events so that their visit to the East End is done in a high-energy, 360 degree constant sweep around.

So, a Doctor driven mad by having to endure the sub-drama antics of a bunch of life haters and forced into wearing a neck brace because nobody stands still there for more than two seconds at a time. Yep, that's certainly on a par with turning baddies into trees and whatever it was she was intending to do with the Loyhargil.

Roundels

In *The Day of the Doctor*, the three Doctors wonder aloud just what the 'round things' that adorn the TARDIS walls are for. If the Rani's TARDIS is anything to go by they're basically little cupboards. A time machine that is dimensionally transcendental is all very well, but when you need to lay your hands on, say, the tool kit or whatever book you're reading at the moment, wandering through endless corridors in search of the library or the tool kit room (or even the shed, we've seen there's a garden of sorts aboard the TARDIS, so presumably there's some kind of shed down there somewhere) takes up far more time than even a Time Lord is prepared to invest. So, handy little cupboards all over the console room walls are a perfect solution.

Although if, as we've seen, the Rani has a Cyberman in one roundel and a Time Lord in another, both at head height, what about the ones underneath? Is she, as the flying heads of the first and second Doctors would indicate, decapitating her specimens and putting them away for safe keeping? The appearances of both creatures later in the adventure would indicate not. So, presumably the roundels below head height offer convenient access to the Cyberman's chest panel (for play with gold) and the Time Lord's genitals (don't ask). It's hardly a sensible use of space. Then there's the fact that to do so, you'd need to hollow out the space behind all the other roundels and somehow squeeze each specimen though the uppermost one and angle them so that they fall upright into the space beyond. It all seems unnecessarily complex, when she could, after all, just as easily bung them into an anteroom, but let us remember, this is the same woman who invested a colossal amount of effort into building an ornate, marble-bedecked headquarters on Lakertya when a simple mobile rocket launcher would suffice.

Women, eh?

Jumping through Time like Hurdlers in a Tizzy

This is the very thing that 'timey wimey' was invented for. Look, we know that in a book which sets out to explain the theories and ideas which drove the characters during the seventh

Doctor's era to do the things they did, you'd be hoping for an explanation as to just how the Rani manages to flash between the Doctor's various incarnations and at the same time somehow have his companion copy the same trick, but for the life of us we can't figure out how.

The Doctor's explanation about jumping time grooves is as good as any, so as far as he's concerned, we're happy enough to go along with that. After all, Ace manages to understand it, although it's more likely that her puny earth brain simply can't process the implications of such temporal mechanics. Neither, as it turns out, can we, but it makes a certain kind of sense and, given the events of *The Space Museum*, there's a precedent.

Not Before She Cloned Me!

Look at events in *The Day of the Doctor* – Clara is able to be present at all points in the Doctor's time stream. In doing so, she can appear anywhere, with any Doctor. Not because she's a constant presence throughout his entire life but because like the Scaroth in *City of Death*, she's been fractured throughout time. The Doctor's other companions underwent a similar fate, thanks to the Rani's device and so they too are fractured across the Doctor's time stream. Whenever the Doctor jumps a time groove, so do his many companions and a fragment of one of them is brought forth to accompany the Doctor because at all times when in Albert Square he had 'a companion' with him. Thus, the device selects at random one of the many fragments of companion to appear alongside the Doctor.

It's simple really.

Less simple is how, later, we see multiple companions at the same time. So, um, the device was overcompensating for the multitude of companions and occasionally, randomly, threw up one or more because it was unable to cope in real time (that is to say the real time that exists in its own reality) with transplanting a single fragment with the frequency that the Doctor's time jumps demanded.

Yes, that'll do. And if you don't agree, write your own book about it. We'll all buy one, so that's six copies sold right there.

Of course the Doctor has at various times had more than one companion with the Fifth Doctor having three. So this being the case, any time we see the Doctor with one companion, the other two companion fragments may still be hanging around, but just not fully formed. This would mean that in say, *Delta and the Bannermen*, Goronwy is a manifestation of the Doctor's absent companion, as is Ray. In *The Happiness Patrol* we have Earl Sigma and Susan Q and in *Greatest Show in the Galaxy* we have Mags and the Stallslady.

Pat Butcher, Colin Baker, Perigosto Stick Maker

That Pat Butcher can't see an Ogron bearing down on her is largely understandable; the poor love has to put up with that every day she looks in a mirror. So, her inability to see the Doctor's enemies filling up Albert Square can be put down to her thinking she had one too many gin and tonics in the Vic and has caught a glimpse of herself reflected in a shop window.

But the Rani's scheme goes deeper – none of the residents of Albert Square can see the alien invaders. Why?

Again, the answer is simple; they're not really there – the monsters are projections of those stored in the Rani's cupboards. After all the time and effort squeezing them into those tiny little holes, there was no way she was going to go through the whole process in reverse, particularly given the sense of urgency now that the Doctor appears to have cottoned on to her plan. It must have taken ages to get that Tractator through such a tiny hole, so presumably once he's in there, he's in there for good. So instead, images of monsters are beamed directly onto the visual cortex of the Doctor and his companions. The only real baddie the Doctor has to face is the Rani herself; the rest are mere projections. Their weapons are projections on projections.

Or it's just a load of made-up stupid shite.

Phone Numbers for Mandy and Big Ron:

Mandy 0891 114455

Big Ron 0891 114466

Phone **NOW!**

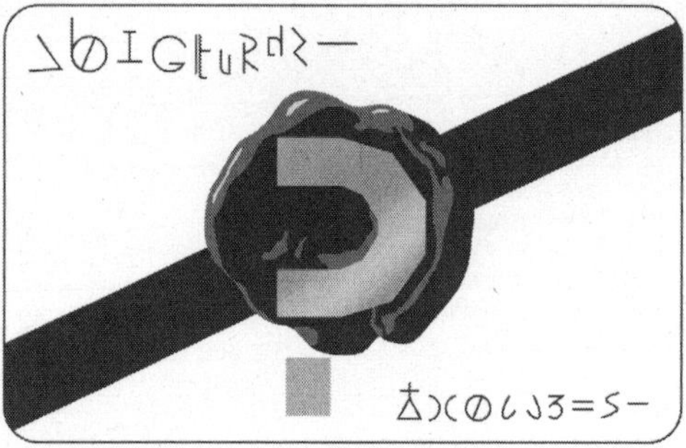

1996 – *The TV Movie*

France perform the last atomic bomb test, Deep Blue beats Gary Kasparov, Nintendo release the N64, OJ Simpson goes on trial, accused of murdering his wife and Steve Jobs' company NeXt is purchased by his previous company Apple in a not remotely dubious or incestuous deal. Legendary Indian stuntwoman Fearless Nadia dies, as do Saul Bass, Timothy Leary, Gene Kelly, Beryl Reid and Jon Pertwee. The highest grossing US film was **Independence Day**. Inexplicably the 12th highest grossing film was **Space Jam**.

1996 – *The TV Movie*

Amid a flurry of florid time puns, Paul McGann debuts as the 8th Doctor, but unexpectedly, and let's face it, it was a brave move, American co-producer Philip Segal ensures Sylvester McCoy gets to pass on the baton.

Arriving in Vancouver in 1999, the Doctor spills the Master's goo and it interferes with the news broadcasts and firework displays. *Nothing else happens.*

What's *that* All Aboot?

Our final glimpse of the Seventh Doctor is when he is on holiday in Vancouver, getting shot. As it was such a serious moment in the Doctor's lifetime there is little comedic value to be mined from the event, although the Doctor's pre-regenerative gurning warrants a mention. It seems an odd turn of events for the Doctor to have developed this habit for this particular regeneration and it isn't clear what's causing it. We did wonder if it was some form of pre-regenerative constipation, but even if it was there really isn't much that the Doctor can do to ease the discomfort. Think about it – he's stuck in an unfamiliar city, and he wouldn't really know what laxative products there were available here. Perhaps syrup of figs would be the best bet to help avoid this sort of thing… please tell us your favourite cure for a backed up bum by visiting our Facebook page.

What we would like to know about this adventure though is just how he managed to get the TARDIS pimped up so nicely? In all of the previous thirty-three years of adventures, the Doctor has travelled around in a ship that looks like it has been cobbled together with old egg boxes and switches from scrapped Vauxhall Vivas, but we see here that he has a rather spiffing new TARDIS that appears to be much more intricate, detailed and just much better made than before. So how did this happen? Did the Doctor win some money on the Lottery and decide to put it to good use and tidy the place up, or is this in fact a new TARDIS that he has nicked? We know from past experience that he has a habit of pilfering these things. Or maybe he took part in an episode of **Changing Rooms** and allowed Laurence Llewllyn-Bowen (A sort of Dapol Eight Doctor made flesh) to have his wicked way with his 'wife'…?

It's all rather nice but we can't help thinking that the Doctor's TARDIS should really look like Steptoe's front room. Things should be a little more shambolic and random than the über-designed new gaff that he lives in here.

Anyway, once he regenerates it all goes to shit. So there our story nearly ends.

1996 – 2005

This wasn't the end for the Seventh Doctor. Thanks to Big Finish, Virgin Books and BBC Books, he and the other Doctors live on, still having adventures.

For that era of **Doctor Who** we thank Sylvester McCoy, Bonnie Langford, Sophie Aldred, John Nathan-Turner and Andrew Cartmel. They made it fresh again.

Further reading on this era is available from Miwk Publishing:

Afterword

'Dementia in Time'

The book you've just leafed through (and regretted paying money for) was produced for charity.

Our chosen charity this time is Alzheimer's Society.

Alzheimer's/dementia/senility are all things which, for as long as I was growing up, were treated as humorous in the media. Sitcom characters could be daffy, forgetful, and violently cantankerous in their old age. In Auton we even made fun of William Hartnell a few times and his forgetfulness.

The truth of the matter is, from the outside the confusion of another can seem amusing. When Frank's mum Mo was diagnosed with Alzheimer's in **EastEnders** there was divided opinion in the press and indeed the playground as to whether the depiction of Mo's downfall was realistic or silly.

Sadly it was both as I found out the hard way.

My grandmother, Bessie Irene Pleasants (she hated the name, consequently hated any **Doctor Who** story with Pertwee's car in it. But loved Pertwee) was a huge part of my life, just as most people's grandparents are. There's something fascinating about seeing your parents deal with their parents. It shows you that the shit you get from mum and dad is just them slinging the same shit that they got from their mum and dad. I do the same now

with my daughter. 'Tidy your room!'
'Why?'
'Because **I** said so!'

We knew her as 'Nan'. Nan was probably the most generous person I've ever encountered and utterly selfless. Finding herself as the single parent of two girls she worked incredibly hard to support them. She would often show me her savings books (she saved every last piece of paper that crossed her letterbox) where she would be paying sometimes just a handful of change into her mortgage. She impressed upon me and my sister the importance of the security of your own home. Retain a roof over your head, nothing else matters. Dinner can be boring, but at least you own the house you're eating it in. Any time she had a few quid left over she put it into the mortgage meaning that she paid it off pretty quickly.

By the time I came around in the late seventies she was already in full control of her finances. She'd helped my mum and dad to buy their place, and she was always there to write a cheque (and then balance it fastidiously in the back of the chequebook) for a school trip, school uniform, Christmas presents, **Star Wars** toys. We had a secure childhood. That's not to say my mum and dad didn't work hard too. My dad seemed to me to be a workaholic. Nan helped out with the 'other' things. Mum and dad would provide food, shelter, heat – all the essentials. Nan was there for the treats I suppose.

From a very early age, every Saturday morning was spent at my nan's house. We'd drive over there (only fifteen minutes), arrive around 8.30am, sometimes do weekly food shopping, be home in time for a roast lunch and then leave around 1pm. Every week without fail. We never questioned this because we liked going. Nan always occupied us either with sweets, making fires in the back garden, cleaning the birdbath, baking (she taught me to cook) and her most prized and amazing possession – the VHS recorder she purchased around 1981 when I was only 4. I remember its arrival so well for two reasons. Firstly I'd never seen a tape that big. I remember my first blank VHS tape in its rigid plastic Polaroid case. So much weight to them back then before the lightweight, cheaper tapes arrived later on. The other reason was that she would record 3hrs worth of entertainment for my sister and I to watch on Saturday. This meant that as well as sit-coms, films, gameshows and cartoons we'd also get to watch **Doctor Who**. I saw the entire Davison era on VHS.

She'd re-use the same tape pretty much every week so occasionally when you'd finished a story, the tape would play through static and then the final moments of say *Black Orchid* would be revealed underneath *Terminus*.

We kept one story from those days, I still have the tape now, not that I expect it even plays. It was the four episode version of *The Five Doctors* and I've watched it so many times I can recite the entire script verbatim. Test me one day.

The remote control for the video was a plug-in job and sometimes you could accidentally lean on it and record over what you were watching. This meant that at three points in that VHS **Saturday Superstore** or **Going Live** would cut in very briefly.

1. 'Charming spot, Doctor'
2. 'I hope you got your sums right'
3. 'No! There's nothing here to harm us'

It was my nan who took me to see *The Ultimate Adventure* in Wimbledon, Space Adventure in Tooley Street, to Balham to visit relatives where the bridge was covered in Dalek bumps.

As I say, she taught me to cook. She was a natural. She would make 3-4 fruit cakes per week and use them as currency in the butcher's, greengrocer's and with friends and neighbours. Need a washing line put up? It'll cost you a fruitcake. She taught me the basics of a roast dinner, she introduced me to tea, the importance of buying in bulk when you can, and that a sell by date was nothing to be afraid of.

When I got my first Saturday job working in the local greengrocer's clearing the week's build-up of rotting fruit and veg and old boxes, she'd be up at 5.30am to ensure I had a cooked breakfast before I was at work for 6am.

The week that *Silver Nemesis* aired, we heard she had breast cancer. I wasn't terribly aware of cancer as a disease or the consequences of it but I did notice it weakened her. She lost weight, acquired a stoop as she walked and was often very uncomfortable.

But she was so bloody strong and robust that she simply didn't let it get the better of her, even though it came back three times over the next twenty years, never really going away at all and always spreading somewhere else. She never let it get the better of her. By the time I was old enough to drive I'd give her a lift to the Royal Marsden (a hospital seemingly made of saints) for the latest check-up and she'd grab her latest sack full of pills, offering me a choice of painkillers if I needed any. Often we'd go straight from the check-up to buy her shopping.

Nan's freezer was a sight to behold. She loved ice lollies, especially Big Feasts and Cornettos. Her freezer was full of them. But as she said, she didn't smoke or drink so they were her only vice. Those and tea which she'd get through easily fifteen-to-twenty cups of per day. I have no idea how her bladder could stand it.

So shopping trips evolved from Sainsburys to either Iceland or later Makro where she could stock up on ice creams for a week's supply.

Eventually I met my wife and got married. Nan was there at the wedding, paying for some of it of course, and we presented her with a bouquet of flowers always in her two favourites colours: green and purple. It was an amazing day, and was one of the few times she posed for a photograph. It was the last photo I'd have with her.

Jo (my wife) and I had been having trouble with money and the flat we were living in and so, because nan had recently fallen victim to a scam whereby a guy had driven her to the building society and made her draw out £5k, we moved in with her.

She welcomed this and was looking forward to it. We cleared out my mum and aunt's old rooms and made space for Jo and I to live without upheaval to nan's routine.

On the first night we were there, we were just about to go to bed when she came in and asked when Jo would be going home. I told her we were married, so we were both staying there. Nan refused to accept we were married. I thought she was joking at first, but then she started getting quite nasty about it. She shouted, was rude to Jo and said she wouldn't have her under her roof.

I was struck dumb. Jo hadn't really had a chance to speak to her before, and I'd always said how much I loved her and what a great person she was. I'd bigged my nan up and there was no evidence of it here. Jo was so upset. I felt terrible. We had nowhere else to go. What I didn't realise at the time, is that Jo recognised my nan's behaviour because she'd seen the same thing in her dad.

The following morning I crept downstairs ready for the fall-out and there wasn't any. She asked if we'd slept well and was as nice as pie. I assumed she'd thought better of it. But I still asked her about last night and she refused to acknowledge it. I thought she was doing it because she felt silly, but I tried to impress upon her that it would mean a lot to Jo if she apologised and cleared the air. She wouldn't have it, she refused to accept that anything had happened the night before. Something just wasn't right.

From this point on we had seven long, horrible months living with my nan. We'd creep about like ninjas, try not to spoil her routine and most important of all, kept quiet. Any noise and she'd be in asking what was going on.

This was not typical of her behaviour before. Something had definitely changed.

It took some time and several trips to the doctor to establish that she was in the early stages of Alzheimer's. I wasn't familiar with the condition really, short of Mo's experiences on **EastEnders**.

Everything about her had changed. She couldn't remember how to cook. She couldn't remember the ingredients for her fruitcake or if she did, she'd make one and forget to turn the over on or worse still, turn the gas on and forget to light it. Cups of unfinished and half-made tea would be dotted around the house, taps would be left on as would the TV. Plugs would be pulled out of the freezer, the door left open, all windows opened for no apparent reason. Really silly things like leaving a loaf of bread outside our door each day 'in case we needed one' became a routine whereby she'd go out to get the bread especially, even in the rain. It almost sounds funny but it's not. It's horrible, it's frightening and worst of all, it takes over everything to the point where you feel they're doing it deliberately to annoy you. Like the time she carried my keyboard and printer out into the garden and left them in the rain. I was livid. 'Why did you do that?!' I yelled, pointlessly.

Caught in the moment you ask a silly question, but the simple fact is, my nan didn't do anything. Alzheimer's did it. Alzheimer's made all those cups of tea, melted the lollies, left the taps running, was rude to the postman, smashed a window, woke me up in the middle of the night because the kitchen was full of blackbirds… it was all Alzheimer's and what it took me a long time to realise was that my nan had gone. She wasn't there anymore. Alzheimer's had taken her over and while it still looked like her, it wasn't her.

Very very rarely she would emerge. You would get a moment of clarity and those moments seem even more precious now than they ever did then. We were in the garden and she was reminiscing about the fox that used to eat plates of dog food she left out. She talked about Saturday mornings and what we had for breakfast (scotch pancakes and lemon curd – still one of my favourites). She asked about my sister, about Jo, about my job. Just before she turned and went back indoors, she said 'Sorry about earlier'.

I still have no idea what she was referring to but it felt as though she knew she wasn't there all the time.

The last time she had a moment of clarity was on Tuesday September 11th 2001.

She came in while I was waiting for my dial-up Freeserve modem to download a photo or something and said 'A plane's flown into a building in New York'.

By this stage I was used to these moments, but I turned the telly on to humour her and sure enough – there it was. And within seconds of me turning it on, almost live footage as I remember, a second plane flew into the other tower. We sat there for three hours watching events unfold. She was clear for the whole time. We theorised, tried to empathise and analysed. Most people remember September 11th, but I remember it for wholly different and all the more selfish reasons.

We moved out in November 2001, handing over to carers who could better handle her erratic behaviour. She worsened over the course of a year and died in December 2002, shortly after my wife found out she was pregnant with our first child.

The circumstances surrounding her death are peculiar to say the least, and I wouldn't wish to take any more dignity from her than Alzheimer's already has. But I categorically believe that Alzheimer's was responsible.

Alzheimer's takes a person, removes their good traits and hides them from you. It then takes the worst elements of their personality and magnifies them, dancing a now empty, confused manifestation of the person you loved around like a puppet. It strips them of all dignity and worse, it can make you resent them.

My father-in-law suffered the same way which made my wife's experiences so much worse in the time we lived at my nan's house. She became a prisoner, working nights and trying to sleep during the day while my nan yelled at people, smashed pans and did all sorts. She would be so diplomatic, so understanding and so patient with this horrible old woman. Because that's what my nan had become. For most of those seven months we were there she was a horrible, horrible person. She could be cruel, a trait I'd never seen in her before.

Alzheimer's was responsible and Alzheimer's is an invisible

disease. It doesn't really debilitate someone physically like cancer, it can be missed so easily.

Research is needed. Someone needs to find what causes this deterioration and prevent it. I wouldn't be so optimistic as to expect a cure, but a preventative treatment would mean no one has to go through what I, my wife and thousands of others go through each year.

Alzheimer's Society is there to improve the quality of life of those suffering with the disease. All charity begins at home, and all charity is often personal. In buying this book, you've donated to Alzheimer's Society and helped them to help someone else.

I can't thank you enough for that. I know my nan would feel the same way. It's a shame you never met her. My wife didn't, and nor did my daughter.

Thank you for buying our book.

Matt West, June 2014

http://www.alzheimers.org.uk/

COMING SOON FROM MIWK PUBLISHING

TIME &
SPACE
& TIME

TRUTHLESS BILGE
ABOUT EVERY
DOCTOR WHO
STORY EVER
BY **ROBERT**
HAMMOND

ISBN 978-1-908630-71-1

ALSO AVAILABLE FROM MIWK PUBLISHING

JN-T

THE LIFE & SCANDALOUS TIMES OF

John Nathan-Turner (signature)

For more than a decade, John Nathan-Turner, or 'JN-T' as he was often known, was in charge of every major artistic and practical decision affecting the world's longest-running science fiction programme, **Doctor Who**. Richard Marson brings his dramatic, farcical, sometimes scandalous and often moving story to life with the benefit of his own inside knowledge and the fruits of over 100 revealing interviews with key friends and colleagues. The author has had access to all of Nathan-Turner's surviving archive of paperwork & photos, many of which appear here for the first time.

"Extraordinary. A great piece of work. I read it in two days' flat, I couldn't stop. I've never seen a biographer enter the story like that, it was brilliant and invigorating. It really is a major piece of **Doctor Who** history and the history of an entire industry."

Russell T. Davies (Writer/Producer)

ISBN 978-1-908630-13-1

ALSO AVAILABLE FROM MIWK PUBLISHING

SCRIPT DOCTOR

The Inside Story of **Doctor Who** 1986-89

by Andrew Cartmel

Andrew Cartmel was the script editor on **Doctor Who** from 1986 to 1989. During his time on the show he introduced the seventh Doctor and his companion Ace (Sylvester McCoy and Sophie Aldred) and oversaw forty-two scripts written by eight writers new to the series.

With a clear mission to bring proper science fiction back into **Doctor Who**, he formulated what was later termed 'The Cartmel Masterplan', re-introducing the mystery to the character of the Doctor as the series celebrated its twenty-fifth anniversary and beyond.

Script Doctor is his memoir of this time based on his diaries, written sometimes on set and sometimes not even in the diary itself but on the back of scripts. This book is illustrated with 32 pages of photographs, many never published before. It is a vivid account of life in the **Doctor Who** production office in the late eighties.

ISBN 978-1-908630-68-1

COMING SOON FROM **MIWK PUBLISHING**

AUTON

SHOCK AND AWE : THE BEST OF 1989-1998

DARK DISPATCHES FROM THE DOCTOR WHO WILDERNESS YEARS -

THE TWISTED WORLD OF FANDOM'S BLACKEST SHEEP

In 1989 Robert Hammond and Daniel Vickery started their own fanzine. **Auton** was an A5 glossy litho-printed 'zine mixing humour, fan fiction and silliness in unequal measures that gained writers Matt West and Chris Orton (among others) along the way, a legion of faithful like-minded readers, and numerous rave **DWM** reviews. And as the years went by **Auton** reflected the impatience of fandom. Early on it was nice, quiet, gently amusing. By the end it was raging, swearing, drunken and fuming.

Take a heap of childishness and swearing, add them to the **Blue Peter** Annual, give it a **Doctor Who** theme and you have £19.99 worth of fun. The **Auton** book contains nearly 85% new material and 15% of old tat from the first 19 issues of this irreverent **Doctor Who** fanzine.

Auton - taking pot-shots at all eras of **Doctor Who** from 1963 right up to the finale of Matt Smith's last season, all in glorious full colour and illustrated throughout.

That advert about the reprint for **Auton - Shock & Awe** on the previous page?

We're only joking.

ADVERTISEMENT

Shangri-La

**Shangri-La Holiday Village
Barry Island,
South Wales**
*Telephone: Wales 234/43
Telex: 95874*

How to get there
By RAIL from London. Through fast trains from London Paddington, to Barry, changing at Cardiff. By COACH. From London Coach Station, each Saturday, departing at about 1p.m. direct to Shangri-La. Returning London at around 1p.m.
Journey time around 6 hours. By ROAD. Visitors travelling by road should make for the turning on the A3290 at Reading, which is 90 miles east of London. Then proceed for 123 miles to the village.

Shangri-La is set amid the lovely Welshcountryside close to a long stretch of sand dunes, which gives on to a wide beach. Being particularly convenient for Londoners it is a holiday location already well known to thousands of visitors from the capital but, like all the locations in this brochure, Shangri-La, with its array of natural and Shangri-La-built amenities is geared to attract people from all parts of this country and abroad.

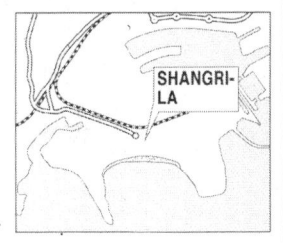

The chalet accomodation is all quite recently built (Shangri-La was opened in 1952) and the standard of furnish-ings is high. All chalets have a living room with fully equipped kitchenette (see illustration overleaf) and a settee converts into a double bed in addition to one or two separate bedrooms as required. All chalets have a private bathroom and toilet and, in common with all locations in this brochure, electricity meters are installed for lighting, heating, cooking and hot water. There is also a coin-operated television receiver.

Dominating the village is the vast "Barry" building which, in addition to providing a reception hall and offices, is the focal point of the village. At night this vast building takes on a more festive air as a high-rated evening of entertrainments gets under way. A resident band plays for dancing in the ballroom, two separate club bars spring to life and small group music, cabaret and resident acts get everyone into the party spirit.

NEW FROM **MIWK PUBLISHING**

MIWK MILK

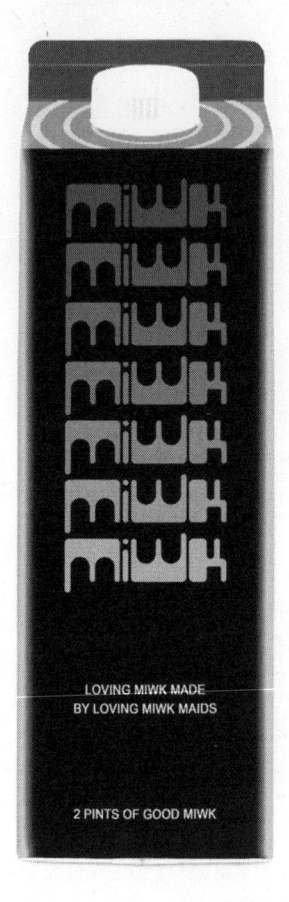

Solid, reliable, reusable glass carton, **really** cool label, reasonably priced, sourced from the fattest cows by the fattest farmers.

DRINK. OUR. **MIWK**.

COMING SOON FROM **MIWK PUBLISHING**

THE NEW ADVENTURES

REPRINTS

DOCTOR WHO: War Drobe by Andrew Cartmel

The Doctor has had enough of his question mark tank top. It's time for change.

And not a moment too soon.

With the help of the Wardrobe of Rassilon and Coat Hangers of Omega, the Other finds himself trapped in a never-ending run of costume changes, each more hideous than the last. Build High for Happiness, Dig Deep for Socks.

DOCTOR WHO: Knicker Raft by Ben Aaronovitch

The Doctor and Benny are stranded by a river - their only hope of escape is to build a massive raft from old knickers, mysteriously left at an altar by local Lizard People.

DOCTOR WHO: Cold Eight by Graeme Curry

The Doctor does battle against a lone, desperate Blizzard Octopus determined to exact revenge for what happened on Tonky Plink VIII.

ALSO AVAILABLE FROM MIWK PUBLISHING

THE QUEST FOR PEDLER
THE LIFE AND IDEAS OF DR KIT PEDLER

by Michael Seely

For many people, Kit Pedler is best remembered as the man who created the Cybermen for **Doctor Who**, a real life scientist who was brought in to act as an advisor and bring some science to the fiction. The Cybermen were his ultimate scientific horror: where the very nature of a man was altered by himself, by his own genius for survival, creating a monster. Pedler was that rare animal, a scientist with an imagination. He liked to think 'What if...?'

Before his premature death in 1981, he had just finished a documentary series for ITV called **Mind Over Matter**, which was the first serious look at the world of the paranormal through the eyes of his enquiring and rational, but imaginative mind.

With contributions from his family, friends, colleagues and critics, this book tells the story behind a fascinating, charismatic, complicated, and demanding human being; a natural teacher who didn't just want to pontificate about the problems facing the world in a television or radio studio, but actually do something practical about them.

Last few hardbacks available,
paperback coming December 2014

ALSO AVAILABLE FROM MIWK PUBLISHING

UNNATURAL SELECTION
The Natural History of The Natural History of Fear

by Jim Mortimore

There is a modern phraseology which defines an item as 'Marmite'. You either categorically dislike something or you evangelically adore it. Jim Mortimore's play *The Natural History of Fear* has frequently been described in such terms. It pushed the envelope of audio drama and it played with the traditional format of storytelling. But it was also declared by actor Paul McGann to be '... the best **Doctor Who** script I've read.'

This book charts the inception of that script from the initial image of the spinning top, through to a brief existence as a book and then to its final realisation as an audio play. It shows the work that goes into producing a set of scripts and the effort that a writer, producer, director, sound engineer, musician and cast go to in order to produce a single play.

In this age of digital piracy and devalued creativity not just in the world of books but in music, film and all manner of art, the currency of a single idea has never been better realised and the creative process more clearly laid out.

As an evolution of a script it is fascinating, not least because it is the evolution of such a fascinating script.

**Last few hardbacks available,
paperback coming December 2014**

www.miwk.com/

www.facebook.com/MiwkPublishingLtd

www.twitter.com/#!/MiwkPublishing